# 365 DAILY PSALMS & PRAYERS

CONTRIBUTING WRITERS:

Christine A. Dallman

Randy Petersen

Publications International, Ltd.

**Christine A. Dallman** is a freelance writer living near Everett, Washington. She is the author of *Daily Devotions for Seniors,* an inspirational resource for maturing adults, as well as coauthor of several other Publications International, Ltd., titles.

**Randy Petersen** is a writer and church educator from New Jersey with more than 40 books to his credit, including *Daily Dose of Knowledge: Bible; God's Answers to Tough Questions;* and *Why Me, God?* A prolific creator of church curriculum, he's also a contributor to the *Quest Study Bible,* the *Revell Bible Dictionary,* and the iLumunia Bible software.

**Illustrations:** Art Explosion; Brand X Pictures; iStockphoto; Jupiterimages Unlimited; Photodisc; PIL Collection; Shutterstock

Louis Weber, CEO
Publications International, Ltd.
7373 North Cicero Avenue
Lincolnwood, Illinois 60712

Permission is never granted for commercial purposes.

ISBN-13: 978-1-4508-6593-7
ISBN-10: 1-4508-6593-3

Manufactured in China.

8 7 6 5 4 3 2 1

# TIMELESS PSALMS AND PRAYERS

*F*or many believers, the Book of Psalms is a favorite Old Testament book because its verses express much of what they feel regarding their relationship with God. Psalms, a collection of 150 poems, was literally ancient Israel's hymnal: Each psalm was written to be set to music for worship. Today, it remains a source of inspiration, comfort, and encouragement as a prayer book for Jews and Christians alike. In fact, the poetry's beauty and power to inspire worship still has modern songwriters spinning melodies around the sacred lyrics of the psalmists.

The purpose of this book is to bring the timeless comfort and inspiration of these psalms to your daily devotions in a unique way. Each of the 366 meditations is designed to help you focus on some aspect of a psalmist's prayer. They include a brief passage from the psalms, a related prayer from a modern-day perspective, and often a final thought or quote that supports the meditation. And while daily entries take only a minute or two to read, the focus of the content is sure to remain with you throughout the day as a source of strength and encouragement.

From page to page, you'll encounter comfort, challenge, and inspiration. Very often you will hear a psalmist's call to trust in God and worship him because of his love, mercy, greatness, or faithfulness. What a wonderful way to begin, end, or interject something uplifting into your day!

With each successive reading, you will be reminded—or perhaps discover for the first time—how relevant these ancient poems are to your own experience. The psalms included in this volume are filled with the cries of real people facing real life issues, just as you face them in your own daily lives.

While the prayers that follow each scripture reading are an echo of the psalmist's heart cry, they bring a more intimate application to each passage. The accompanying prayer is intended to give you a place to begin your own prayer, a prayer that resonates with a sincere and trusting faith and that is free to engage in open and honest conversation with the God who cares deeply for you.

May you be blessed as you enjoy ever-increasing intimacy with the God of the ages over his timeless Word throughout the year ahead!

# JANUARY 1

Come, bless the Lord, all you servants of the Lord,
who stand by night in the house of the Lord!
Lift up your hands to the holy place, and bless the Lord.

Psalm 134:1–2

*I* have received rich blessings from you, dear Lord. I cannot count the ways you have blessed me. But now I'm invited to bless *you*. I love the idea that

I can bring you joy by praising you, by thanking you, and by serving you. Let me pay you compliments for your creativity, wisdom, and patience. I love you, Lord, and I'm deeply grateful that you are my Lord.

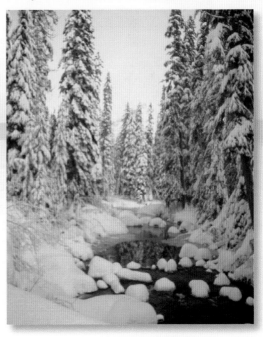

Blessing involves saying and doing. God blesses us by speaking his Word into our lives and by doing things to help us. We bless God by praising and serving him.

# JANUARY 2

Out of my distress I called on the Lord;
the Lord answered me and set me in a broad place.

Psalm 118:5

*I*t's just a matter of time, sovereign Lord, until each struggle I face passes and I emerge from a place of distress into a place of deliverance and rest.

Help me to never abandon hope in the middle of a trial. May I always press on in prayer, calling out to you, knowing that you hear me and that you are orchestrating the outcome for my eternal good. Hear my prayer even now, for I am calling on you for the deliverance I need this day.

More things are wrought by prayer
than this world dreams of.

—Alfred Lord Tennyson,
*The Passing of Arthur*

# JANUARY 3

Open to me the gates of righteousness,
that I may enter through them
and give thanks to the Lord.

Psalm 118:19

*G*lorious Lord, I come before you to worship.
I don't take this privilege lightly. I imagine the
ancient Israelites climbing the steep streets of
Jerusalem toward the Temple and entering through
those beautiful gates. I imagine the priests entering the Holy Place with the sacred incense and holy
bread, and the high priest venturing into the Holy
of Holies. Coming into your presence is a sacred
trust. But I don't have to climb a hill; I can kneel in
my home. You have already opened the gates to your
presence, and you invite me to enter whenever I will.
So, here I am to worship. You are my great God. I
thank you, and I love you.

Therefore, I urge you, brothers and
sisters, in view of God's mercy, to offer
your bodies as a living sacrifice, holy and
pleasing to God—this is your true and
proper act of worship.

—Romans 12:1 (NIV)

# JANUARY 4

*O* God, our help in ages past, our hope for
   years to come,
Our shelter from the stormy blast, and our eternal
   home.
Under the shadow of Thy throne still may we dwell
   secure;
Sufficient is Thine arm alone, and our defense is sure.
Before the hills in order stood, or earth received
   her frame,
From everlasting, Thou art God, to endless years
   the same.

—Isaac Watts,
"O God, Our Help in Ages Past"

Hope is the expectation of
good things to come.

# JANUARY 5

The Lord will give what is good,
and our land will yield its increase.
Psalm 85:12

Almighty Lord, the soil of my soul is daily
gathering the seeds of my thoughts, attitudes, and
deeds. May your own hands weed the soil and cause
only the best to grow as I confess my failings and
give you glory for the good you've sown within me.

# JANUARY 6

Bless the Lord, O my soul,
and all that is within me,
bless his holy name.
Psalm 103:1

With my whole being, precious Lord, I exalt
your wonderful name. Indeed, whenever I hear your
people praise your name, my soul is overwhelmed
with joy, for you are a great God, who is both just
and merciful in all that you do. I bless your holy
name now and forever. Amen.

# JANUARY 7

The boundary lines have fallen for me in pleasant places;
I have a goodly heritage.

Psalm 16:6

*T*hank you, Lord, for the blessings you have bestowed on me. Thank you for the love of my family and for the "extended family" of my circle of friends. Thank you for the work I do each day, whether I get paid for it or not. Thank you for laughter and music and creativity. Thank you for a world rich with wonder. Thank you for the opportunities you have given me to learn and grow, to care and communicate, and to share with others. I think back on all the "coincidences" that have brought me to the place where I am today, and I'm grateful for your hand in them. Those boundary lines don't just *fall* in pleasant places. You put them there. Thank you.

The faithful will abound with blessings.

—Proverbs 28:20

# JANUARY 8

This God—his way is perfect;
the promise of the Lord proves true;
he is a shield for all who take refuge in him.

Psalm 18:30

*G*reat God, I praise and honor you for keeping your promises. You have said that you would be with us always and that you would give us life and peace and protect us from harm. You have acknowledged that tough times would come, but you have promised to meet us there, to share your bountiful resources with us, to help us through the crises, and to be our refuge. Thank you, Lord, for being with us.

Often the Lord has to protect us from our own crazy schemes. We might think we know where we're going and how to get there, but he has a better idea.

# JANUARY 9

For he is our God,
and we are the people of his pasture,
and the sheep of his hand.

Psalm 95:7

*F*ather in Heaven! . . . Grant us to feel that without Thee we can do nothing—a feeling not of cowardly dependence but a feeling of hopeful strength, in the happy assurance that Thou art powerful among the weak.

—Søren Kierkegaard, "Our Dependence on Thee"

# JANUARY 10

O taste and see that the Lord is good;
happy are those who take refuge in him.

Psalm 34:8

*W*hat flavor of your goodness will I taste today, Lord? You are always blessing my life with good things. I savor your grace and mercy. Your love is a feast. I always want seconds of your kindness. And your recipe for peace is not to be outdone by anyone. I am happy to be invited to such a banquet.

# JANUARY 11

Your decrees are very sure;
holiness befits your house,
O Lord, forevermore.

Psalm 93:5

*D*oes holiness befit *my* house, righteous Lord? As I think about the activities that go on in my home, the attitudes displayed, and the priorities represented, is it a holy place? I hope so. That's my desire. Do we put more emphasis on loving you than in acquiring electronic gadgets? Do we love each other rather than fight all the time? Is honesty a hallmark of this home, or do we sneak and hide and deceive and manipulate? Dear Lord, I want a holy home. That's why I dedicate my dwelling place to you. I want *you* to feel at home here.

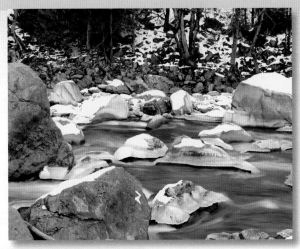

Home is where the heart
is most fully what it is.

# JANUARY 12

Be strong, and let your heart take courage,
all you who wait for the Lord.

Psalm 31:24

*O*, for a faith that will not shrink, though
pressed by every foe,
That will not tremble on the brink of any earthly woe!
That will not murmur nor complain beneath the
chastening rod,
But, in the hour of grief or pain, will lean upon its God.
A faith that shines more bright and clear when
tempests rage without;
That when in danger knows no fear, in darkness
feels no doubt.
Lord, give me such a faith as this, and then,
whate'er may come,
I'll taste, e'en here, the hallowed bliss of an eternal home.

—William H. Bathurst,
"O, For a Faith that Will Not Shrink"

By faith we understand that the worlds
were prepared by the word of God,
so that what is seen was made
from things that are not visible.

—Hebrews 11:3

# JANUARY 13

But may all who seek you rejoice and be glad in you;
may those who love your salvation
say continually, "Great is the Lord!"

Psalm 40:16

*H*eavenly Father, you *are* great! I am truly grateful for your salvation, and as I continually seek you, I rejoice in everything you reveal to me about yourself. I am, indeed, glad in you today. I feel blessed and deeply honored to be here with you, the God of the universe. When I try to think about it, it's a reality that's hard to wrap my mind around, and yet it's true. May I continually be in awe of your greatness and be full of delight when I reflect on who you are and how you have saved me.

If God's greatness is powerfully
evident to us, we can imagine
those around his throne in heaven
continually worshipping him.

# JANUARY 14

For a day in your courts is better than a thousand elsewhere.
I would rather be a doorkeeper in the house of my God
than live in the tents of wickedness.

Psalm 84:10

Almighty Father, the ways of the world offer a dose of short-lived fun, followed by a sentence of long-term sorrow. Please keep me from "buying in" to the world's lies. Help me focus my intentions and desires on the path of life to which you call me. It may not seem glamorous at a temporal glance, but the wonders and joys you offer are deep and pure and profound, lasting for all eternity and satisfying the true desires of my heart. Thank you for the peace and promise of living in your presence.

The ways of the world are those that look like candy but turn out to be the bitterest of pills. The ways of Christ, on the contrary, may seem a bitter pill in the beginning, but they lead us to an exquisite feast.

# JANUARY 15

I kept my faith, even when I said,
"I am greatly afflicted."

Psalm 116:10

Lord, I don't understand my suffering, but I will choose to trust you anyway. You are my strength and deliverer. I praise you with all my heart. For you are my rock in times of trouble.

# JANUARY 16

Happy are the people who know the festal shout, who walk, O Lord, in the light of your countenance; they exult in your name all day long, and extol your righteousness.

Psalm 89:15–16

God of joy, you fill my heart with good things. You bestow your loving smile upon me and satisfy my longings. Life is full of blessings when I live each day in your presence. Thank you for the joy you bring to me. Help me share that joy with others.

# JANUARY 17

You are a hiding place for me;
you preserve me from trouble;
you surround me with glad cries of deliverance.

Psalm 32:7

*D*ear Lord, it's a jungle out there. Everyone's rushing to meet their own needs, oblivious to anyone else's. People can be downright mean. They insult and slander me. Even when people act nicely, I always wonder how sincere they are. Are they just waiting for me to slip up? But, Lord, I know I can come to you for genuine support. When life is at its craziest, let me hide in you for a while. Speak peace to me with your Spirit. Surround me with others who know what I'm going through. Heal me and renew my energy.

Hiding can either be bad or good in the Bible. After Adam and Eve disobeyed God, they hid from him in the Garden, but Rahab did well to hide the Israelite spies in Jericho. Hiding *from* God is a major problem, but when we flee from harm by hiding *in* God, it's truly a blessing!

# JANUARY 18

For the Lord God is a sun and shield; he bestows favor and honor. No good thing does the Lord withhold from those who walk uprightly.

Psalm 84:11

*L*ord God, help me walk uprightly today—not to impress anyone else or to make myself feel morally superior to those around me. Help me walk uprightly that I might enjoy fellowship with you as you intend it so that nothing may hinder our joy of communing together throughout the day. If others see your light shining in me, may they be drawn to you. If your blessing comes through an act of love or obedience, give me a thankful heart that you have upheld me in your righteousness. Grant me true humility as you teach me to walk in your ways. It is because you are good that I can walk with you. Thank you for all of your blessings!

Attribute to God all that is good, and walk in his goodness as in the light of a beacon to which you can quickly point if someone notices how bright your way is.

# JANUARY 19

Let your steadfast love, O Lord, be upon us,
even as we hope in you.

Psalm 33:22

*D*ear Father, I long to live in a nation that looks to you and walks in ways of truth and love, ways that lead to peace and authentic unity among those who hope in you. Please renew my heart in the things that please you, so I can be the kind of citizen that makes such a nation possible.

# JANUARY 20

As for the holy ones in the land, they are the noble,
in whom is all my delight.

Psalm 16:3

*S*aints are made, not by their own deeds or piety, but by the saving grace of God alone. For only he has the power to redeem us and clothe us with righteousness.

# JANUARY 21

I will come praising the mighty deeds of the Lord God,
I will praise your righteousness, yours alone.

Psalm 71:16

Holy God, I ask for your righteousness to fill me, thrill me, captivate me, and motivate me. I want a righteousness steeped in your love rather than in my own pride. I want a righteous life that emanates a deep sense of gratitude and not a holier-than-thou attitude. This isn't about me being some sort of spiritual giant. It's about you living your life through me. In Jesus' sacred name, I pray. Amen.

We don't find righteousness in good behavior. We find good behavior by relying on the righteousness of Christ.

# JANUARY 22

Father of orphans and protector of widows
is God in his holy habitation.

Psalm 68:5

Heavenly Father, I think of you, the Father of all creation. Yet I realize that there are all kinds of fathers in this world. Some are absent or abusive; some are distant or demanding; and some are caring and giving. When some people think of you as a father, fear and anger consumes them. But here the psalmist calls you "father of orphans." For anyone who needs a good father, you step in. Whatever failings any earthly father has, you make up for that earthly father. In you, there is genuine fatherly love available to us all. Thank you, my "heavenly dad."

Religion that is pure and undefiled before God, the Father, is this: to care for orphans and widows in their distress, and to keep oneself unstained by the world.

—James 1:27

# JANUARY 23

Commit your way to the Lord;
trust in him, and he will act.

Psalm 37:5

I am trusting Thee, Lord Jesus,
Trusting only Thee;
Trusting Thee for full salvation,
Great and free.

—Frances R. Havergal,
"I Am Trusting Thee, Lord Jesus"

# JANUARY 24

O come, let us worship and bow down,
let us kneel before the Lord, our Maker!

Psalm 95:6

A bent knee is a form of worship that may or may not be accompanied by a humble heart. I can pray that my heart will be right with God, however, even as I bend my knee. May God grant me the heart of a true worshipper!

# JANUARY 25

Glorious are you, more majestic
than the everlasting mountains.

Psalm 76:4

*W*e salute the kings of the earth with "Your
Majesty." How much more worthy are you of that
honor than they, Lord! How regal are your works,
such as the mountains! How they reflect your own
majestic nature! And yet in another sense, they can
reflect only dimly, for I'm aware that a full revelation
of your glory would be my undoing. Thank you that
you show me, though, what you are like in ways that
I can perceive and to which I can respond. These
revelations inspire worship and awe in my spirit and
point ahead to the day when you will make me able
to "handle" the unveiling of your majesty as I worship in your very presence.

The truly majestic is found in few things
on earth, and yet when we encounter God's
majesty, we know it immediately, instinc-
tively. It, perhaps more than any other quality, inspires our worship. We must be careful,
then, not to allow ourselves to worship at the
altar of any majesty other than God's own.

24

# JANUARY 26

They are like trees planted by streams of water,
which yield their fruit in its season, and their leaves do not wither.
In all that they do, they prosper.

Psalm 1:3

*N*ourishing Lord, I want to grow in you. Let me drink in your goodness and bear spiritual fruit. This is what I was made for, isn't it? To thrive in an ongoing relationship with you? Speak to me as I come before you each day, not only praying but also listening. Instruct me as I read your Word. Guide me as I live each moment. Use other believers to encourage me and steer me in the right direction. Empower me to touch others with your love. I may be just a sapling now, Lord, but I'm growing— with your help.

The glory of God is a person fully alive.

—Irenaeus

# JANUARY 27

I will sing of your might; I will sing aloud of your steadfast love
in the morning. For you have been a fortress for me
and a refuge in the day of my distress.

Psalm 59:16

Alone with none but thee, my God,
I journey on my way.
What need I fear when thou art near,
O king of night and day?
More safe am I within thy hand
Than if a host should round me stand.

# JANUARY 28

They shall celebrate the fame of your abundant goodness,
and shall sing aloud of your righteousness.

Psalm 145:7

It is a blessing in itself to celebrate God's goodness. The Bible records a number of the faithful
who broke into ecstatic praise when God did good
things in their lives: Moses, Miriam, Hannah, David,
Mary, Elizabeth, and Paul, as well as other apostles.
Go ahead! You're in good company.

# JANUARY 29

He does not deal with us according to our sins,
nor repay us according to our iniquities.

Psalm 103:10

Heavenly Father, I'm still not sure I really understand forgiveness. I know all about right and wrong, and I try to do what's right. I see that misbehavior on my part brings bad results. I'm deeply sorry for the sins I've committed, and I know I deserve your punishment. But instead of punishing me, you forgive. You take the penalty upon yourself, and you invite me to live in a loving relationship with you. You have every right to banish me from your presence, but instead you welcome me in. It is truly amazing! Humbly, I thank you.

Just as I am, Thy love unknown
Hath broken every barrier down;
Now, to be Thine, yea, Thine alone,
O Lamb of God, I come, I come!

—Charlotte Elliot,
"Just As I Am"

# JANUARY 30

O Lord, our Sovereign,
how majestic is your name in all the earth!

Psalm 8:1

The queens and kings of earth borrow their majesty from God's hand. No mortal, with all his might, can cause even a blade of grass to grow, and yet the grandeur of the mountains on which the meadows flourish is the result of a mere few words spoken by the Lord God!

# JANUARY 31

Deliver me from my enemies, O my God;
protect me from those who rise up against me.

Psalm 59:1

When my enemies rise up against me, almighty Father, I'm tempted to ask you to crush and destroy them. But I pray that you would fill my heart with mercy so that, instead of asking for revenge, I will merely ask with the psalmist that you will rescue and protect me from those who seek to harm me, for I belong to you.

# FEBRUARY 1

Surely goodness and mercy shall follow me all the days of my life,
and I shall dwell in the house of the Lord my whole life long.

Psalm 23:6

My loving Lord, I thank you for the past few months with all its joys and struggles. There were delightful moments of love shared with special people. I bask in those memories. Yet there were also challenges—heartaches, losses, and disappointments. As I look back, I recognize that you stayed with me in those tough times. I came to know you in a whole new way. Thank you, Lord, for your care and guidance, step by step, day by day. Your goodness and mercy have indeed followed me. I've been blessed. In Jesus' wondrous name, I pray. Amen.

Eternity isn't just some future promise of a timeless existence. It's a *quality* of life, lived in the embrace of an everlasting God. For the believer, eternal life has already begun. Praise the Lord!

# FEBRUARY 2

One thing I asked of the Lord,
that will I seek after:
to live in the house of the Lord
all the days of my life.

Psalm 27:4

*I* want to be where you are, dear Lord. I always want to be able to hear you—to always be communing with you. "Pray continually," your Word tells

me. Please hold me in that place of prayer. It is prayer that helps keep me near your "throne of grace" throughout the day. Thank you for inviting me here. In your presence—in the house of the Lord—is where I long to abide forever.

Let us then approach God's throne of grace with confidence, so that we may receive mercy and find grace to help us in our time of need.

—Hebrews 4:16 (NIV)

# FEBRUARY 3

You are the God who works wonders;
you have displayed your might among the peoples.

Psalm 77:14

*M*iracles happen every day. It's my perspective that often misses them. Do I see the miracle of sunrise? Of a functioning body? Of a flower blooming or the changing seasons? May the Lord change my perspective so I won't miss the miracles of his provision, protection, and salvation in my life.

# FEBRUARY 4

Let the favor of the Lord our God be upon us,
and prosper for us the work of our hands—
O prosper the work of our hands!

Psalm 90:17

*L*ord God, today I offer thanks for the work you've given me to do and the ability you've given me to do it. I pray that when you put in my hands something that seems beyond my strength or abilities, I would look to you for what I need and trust in your grace and power to work through me.

# FEBRUARY 5

He will redeem me unharmed
from the battle that I wage,
for many are arrayed against me.

Psalm 55:18

*S*ometimes, when I leave my home, heavenly
Father, it feels as if I'm going off to war. Other times,
my home itself seems like a battleground. People
challenge my decisions, they compete with me, they
want this or that from me, they disagree on the silliest things, and they blame me for everything that
goes wrong. And things do go wrong! The wounds
I sustain each day are substantial, and that's why
I come to you today, dear Lord. Please strengthen
me. Shield me from destructive criticism. Bolster
my feelings against the deflating comments I hear.
Give me the confidence I need to do what I'm called
to do. I don't need to win this war, my Lord—just
survive it.

Do not be overcome by evil,
but overcome evil with good.

—Romans 12:21

# FEBRUARY 6

He loves righteousness and justice;
the earth is full of the steadfast love of the Lord.

Psalm 33:5

My heavenly Father, thank you for surrounding me with all the blessings that flow from your love in action—in this world and in my life. As I move through this day, cause me to walk in your righteousness and justice. May your steadfast love steady me as I reach out, not only to those who will be appreciative of your grace but also to those who will not be. For the glory of your name, I pray. Amen.

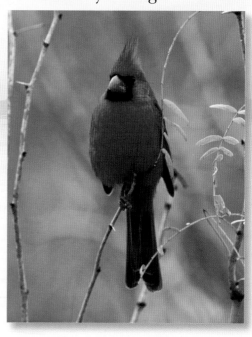

He has showed you, O mortal, what is good.
And what does the Lord require of you?
To act justly and to love mercy and
to walk humbly with your God.

—Micah 6:8 (NIV)

# FEBRUARY 7

From the rising of the sun to its setting
the name of the Lord is to be praised.

Psalm 113:3

Today I will praise you, Lord God. I will leave off my concerns and focus on the many reasons I have to give you thanks and praise. Please fill me with a spirit of worship today. May it even overflow to inspire those around me to see and acknowledge how good and wonderful you are.

# FEBRUARY 8

Lift up your heads, O gates! and be lifted up, O ancient doors!
that the King of glory may come in. Who is the King of glory?
The Lord, strong and mighty, the Lord, mighty in battle.

Psalm 24:7–8

In the ancient world, the victory parade of a conquering king was a spectacular occurrence. We get a meager glimpse of that nowadays when a sports team wins a championship, but the psalmist was pulling out all the stops to welcome the King of Glory.

# FEBRUARY 9

How great are your works, O Lord!
Your thoughts are very deep!

Psalm 92:5

Almighty Father, I want to learn from you. Can you teach me wisdom? I'm not talking about facts and formulas. I want to know how to see the world around me. I want to figure out what's really going on. Too often I'll be talking to someone in need and never know it. Will you teach me how to see that need? Will you make me more sensitive

to people's inner longings? Will you help me sense those moments when a friend needs an encouraging word? Give me your perfect wisdom, dear Lord.

If any of you is lacking in wisdom, ask God, who gives to all generously and ungrudgingly, and it will be given you.

—James 1:5

# FEBRUARY 10

The Lord lives! Blessed be my rock,
and exalted be the God of my salvation.

Psalm 18:46

Is there some way today, awesome God, that you can exalt your name through me? A way I might highlight the blessing of your salvation to those around me? I don't want to preach or push or pry in my desire for people to know how wonderful it is 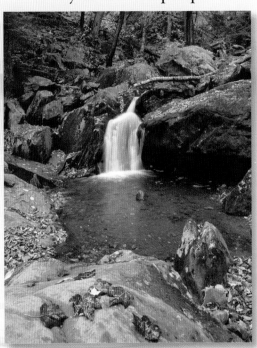 to belong to you. I just want to point to you in some encouraging and helpful way. Exalt yourself through me, I pray, in ways you see fit, in ways you know will be a benefit to those you've placed in my life and to those whom you send across my path.

When humanity is exalted for some accomplishment,
it is not long before it topples from its pedestal.
When God's name is exalted, however, there is no
fear of disillusionment or disappointment.

# FEBRUARY 11

For you, O Lord, have made me glad by your work;
at the works of your hands I sing for joy.

Psalm 92:4

*I* rejoice today, O brilliant Creator, in the glory of what you have made. The sheer majesty of mountains and oceans is awe-inspiring. But it's just as inspiring if I think about the tiniest parts of your creation—an insect's body armor, a plant's growth process, and a strand of human DNA. You have made everything with wit and wonder, including me!

# FEBRUARY 12

For God is the king of all the earth; sing praises with a psalm.
God is king over the nations; God sits on his holy throne.

Psalm 47:7–8

*As* I rejoice in God's greatness today, I am not alone. Heaven continually sings his praises; I join a heavenly host when I sing to him. The earth, too, is full of his glory and thus praises him; I join an earthly host, as well, when I seek to glorify my Lord and King.

# FEBRUARY 13

I will sing to the Lord,
because he has dealt bountifully with me.

Psalm 13:6

*I* know I have a million reasons to sing today, O Lord! Please flood my mind with them even now. I have more reasons to be joyful than to be upset. Would you help me tune my heart and mind to a frequency of praise and worship today and avoid places on my emotional "dial" that tune in to channels of gloom and grumbling? I'll start by praising you for your bountiful grace and love. What would I do without them? Thank you, Father!

O for a thousand tongues to sing
My great Redeemer's praise,
The glories of my God and King,
The triumphs of His grace!

—Charles Wesley,
"O for a Thousand Tongues to Sing"

# FEBRUARY 14

Wake up! Bestir yourself for my defense,
for my cause, my God and my Lord!

Psalm 35:23

*S*overeign Lord, I need your help. I have come to the end of my own ability. You know the situation I'm in, the problems I'm having, and the obstacles I face. I need a miracle! Please step in to help. I've tried to fix things myself, but I've made

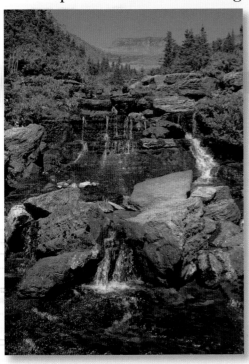

things worse. Whenever I forge ahead in my own direction, I do damage. So I'm appealing to you. I need you now. I've always needed you, but now I realize how much. Don't be a stranger to me. I invite you to step in and work your wonders in my situation. And for whatever I do, I will give you all the glory.

Everyone who calls on the name
of the Lord shall be saved.

—Romans 10:13

# FEBRUARY 15

By day the Lord commands his steadfast love,
and at night his song is with me,
a prayer to the God of my life.

Psalm 42:8

What song of praise can I sing to my Lord and Savior right now that I can carry in my heart and on my lips throughout the day and into the night, and even as I drift off to sleep? It is the song of sincere gratitude.

# FEBRUARY 16

For the Lord loves justice;
he will not forsake his faithful ones.
The righteous shall be kept safe forever.

Psalm 37:28

If I believe God will keep me safe forever, what can my suffering in this life mean? It can only mean that I am not yet home. But God is faithfully leading me there to my eternal haven, keeping me safe from abandoning the path along the way through this sometimes painful but temporal journey.

# FEBRUARY 17

The fear of the Lord is the beginning of wisdom;
all those who practice it have a good understanding.

Psalm 111:10

Great and glorious God, I live in a culture where mocking and disrespect are the norm, even considered a form of humor. How can I begin to understand what it means to fear you and to have reverence and awe for you? O Lord, teach me what this kind of fear is and what it means in attitude and action. I want to learn your wisdom. The wisdom of the world is shallow and can easily collapse, but your wisdom is timeless, irrefutable, a safeguard, and a blessing. Please open my heart and mind more and more to your thoughts and ways.

It is only when men begin to worship
that they begin to grow.

—Calvin Coolidge

# FEBRUARY 18

Save us, we beseech you, O Lord!
O Lord, we beseech you, give us success!
Psalm 118:25

*I*t seems as though everyone is grasping for success. In this dog-eat-dog world, there's plenty of pressure to come out on top. Lord, you know that I want success, too—success in the projects I do each day, in my family life, and in my dealings with others. Grant me success, I pray! But then I wonder, *What is success?* And I need to come back to you for the answer. Grant me *true* success, Lord, not the materialistic success the world offers. But let me be truly effective in doing what you want.

The Hebrew words for "Save us, Lord!" from Psalm 118 form the basis of the *Hosanna* shout offered at the triumphal entry of Jesus. It was a cry of praise, but also a call for help directed to someone with the power to help.

# FEBRUARY 19

Give justice to the weak and the orphan;
maintain the right of the lowly and the destitute.

Psalm 82:3

Great and good Father, increase my concern for those who need practical intervention in their lives and who may need the help of another person to encourage or teach or defend or shelter them in some way. Bring these vulnerable ones to my attention, and though I may not be able to provide everything they need, show me what you would have me offer that would demonstrate your care. Grant me your own compassion and willingness to give of myself for the sake of another. In Jesus' name, I pray. Amen.

As I help others, I cultivate a spirit of helpfulness and love in those around me—in my children, in neighbors, in coworkers, and in my community.

# FEBRUARY 20

I will both lie down and sleep in peace;
for you alone, O Lord, make me lie down in safety.

Psalm 4:8

*I*f I carry my worries with me and never lay them down, even to sleep, I become less and less able to meet the challenges they represent. Worry is a form of self-destruction, while faith is a means of daily renewal.

# FEBRUARY 21

I will sing to the Lord as long as I live; I will sing praise to my God while I have being. May my meditation be pleasing to him, for I rejoice in the Lord.

Psalm 104:33–34

*L*ook upon us, O Lord, and let all the darkness of our souls vanish before the beams of thy brightness. Fill us with holy love, and open to us the treasures of thy wisdom. . . . Then shall our longing be satisfied, and our peace shall be perfect.

—Augustine of Hippo

# FEBRUARY 22

The mighty one, God the Lord,
speaks and summons the earth
from the rising of the sun to its setting.

Psalm 50:1

Almighty God, when you speak, I listen. Why wouldn't I? You are the creator of human life, and I know you are right about how I should live. So keep speaking to me through the Scriptures. Keep nudging me with your Spirit. Bring to my mind those matters you want me to pay attention to. Help me pull away from the TV, the Internet, the cell phone, and the video games, and let me set my focus on you.

In the beginning was the Word, and the Word was with God, and the Word was God. [Jesus] was in the beginning with God. All things came into being through him, and without him not one thing came into being.

—John 1:1–3

# FEBRUARY 23

Seek the Lord and his strength;
seek his presence continually.

Psalm 105:4

Riches I heed not, nor man's empty praise:
  Be thou mine inheritance now and always;
Be thou and thou only the first in my heart;
  O Sovereign of Heaven, my Treasure thou art.
High King of Heaven, thou Heaven's bright sun,
  O grant me its joys
      after victory is won!
Great heart of my own heart, whatever befall,
  Still be my vision, O Ruler of all.

—"Be Thou My Vision,"
a traditional Irish hymn

In seeking only God,
we always find what we need.

46

# FEBRUARY 24

Because your steadfast love is better than life,
my lips will praise you. So I will bless you as long as I live;
I will lift up my hands and call on your name.

Psalm 63:3–4

*D*ear Lord, you know I have choices all the time—what to do, what to say, how to spend my time, and where to spend my money. Sometimes I have to choose between good and bad, but often the options are what's good and what's better. I have to agree with the psalmist that your love is better than life itself. Everything that I would choose to improve my life, to get ahead in life, and to make my life more comfortable or successful or exciting—it all pales in importance when compared to my relationship with you. That's why I praise you, bless you, and rely on you for all I need. Blessed be the name of the Lord.

The Hebrew word translated as "steadfast love" here and throughout the Old Testament (more than 200 times) is *chesed.* Two ideas collide in this word—strength and compassion. It's a deep-felt expression of fierce loyalty. It's a kindness that the person doesn't have to show but wants to.

# FEBRUARY 25

For his anger is but for a moment; his favor is for a lifetime.
Weeping may linger for the night, but joy comes with the morning.

Psalm 30:5

When bad things happen, my Lord, I'm full of questions. Why? If "God is love," and I believe you are, how can you let us suffer like this? It doesn't make sense. I twist and turn it in my mind, and there's no way to make sense of it. If you are Lord of all, and I believe you are, can't you prevent disaster? Or are you punishing us for some reason? I don't get it. But then the dawn breaks with . . . not an answer exactly, but a kind of whisper. "Trust me and love me." You invite me into this lifetime relationship that's based not on understanding but on loving faith. I may never figure you out, Lord, but I'll keep talking with you about it. And please keep whispering to me.

Blessed are those who mourn,
for they will be comforted.

—Matthew 5:4

# FEBRUARY 26

Return, O my soul, to your rest,
for the Lord has dealt bountifully with you.

Psalm 116:7

*B*e devoted to prayer and to listening to God, and he will show you efficiencies and provisions for accomplishing your tasks, ones you never dreamed existed. They will come "out of nowhere" at times, and your amazement and relief will quickly turn into joy and gratitude.

# FEBRUARY 27

O Lord, all my longing is known to you;
my sighing is not hidden from you.

Psalm 38:9

*E*very morning, God's mercy is brand new. He hits the reset button, erasing yesterday's regrets and charting a new course. Don't get bogged down in old long- ings. What is God putting in your heart *today?*

# FEBRUARY 28

My eyes are ever toward the Lord,
for he will pluck my feet out of the net.

Psalm 25:15

My human instincts tell me to keep my eyes on those around me and to look out for what they might be doing or saying that could harm me. But your way, Lord, is counterintuitive; you call me to keep my eyes on you, for you promise to take care of me, keeping me safe. So I have a choice today: I can try to take care of myself, which is a stressful and often unsuccessful means of seeking safety, or I can trust you and enjoy a day of peace in your presence. I'm so thankful that I can choose you today.

If I've stepped into a "net" recently,
I must refuse to focus on my feet.
Turning my eyes heavenward,
I will call on the Lord and
trust him to save me.

# FEBRUARY 29

O send out your light and your truth; let them lead me;
let them bring me to your holy hill
and to your dwelling.

Psalm 43:3

Lead me, dear Lord. I need your light shining on the road ahead of me. Life is complicated these days, and I don't know where to turn. Illuminate the options for me. Let me see which path to take. I need your truth ringing in my ears. So many voices these days woo me this way or that way, I don't know

whom to believe. Except you. I trust your Word, and I trust you to guide me through my current straits.

The Lord went in front of them in a pillar of cloud by day, to lead them along the way, and in a pillar of fire by night, to give them light, so that they might travel by day and by night.

—Exodus 13:21

# MARCH 1

You show me the path of life.
In your presence there is fullness of joy;
in your right hand are pleasures forevermore.

Psalm 16:11

Today, Lord, I've come into your presence again, just to be near you. Whether you have a new insight for me or just a reassurance of your care for me, I'm happy for the opportunity to commune with you right now. Help me stay close to you throughout the day, and please keep your song of joy alive in my heart, fueled by gratitude for all the goodness you bring into my life. You are the one who makes my life truly worthwhile. May I remain in step with you along this blessing-filled path of life.

If we live by the Spirit,
let us also be guided by the Spirit.

—Galatians 5:25

# MARCH 2

My flesh and my heart may fail,
but God is the strength of my heart and my portion forever.
Psalm 73:26

Heavenly Father, in my weak moments when
I fail to be what I should be, when I don't do what
I ought to do, when I say what I shouldn't, and when
I'm silent when I should speak, please intervene! Be
my strength! Redeem my mistakes! Show yourself
strong when I falter, and bring glory to yourself. I
look to you and want to point others to you today.
Use my imperfections to highlight my great need for

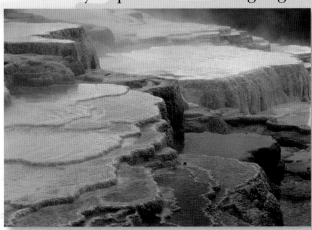

you, and teach
me to walk in
your power
and not in my
own withering
strength.

God generally doesn't seek out the
innately strong as "poster children" for
faith; it is most often the weak through
whom he can best demonstrate his
strength and in whom he can
cultivate great faith.

# MARCH 3

Why are you cast down, O my soul, and why are you disquieted
within me? Hope in God; for I shall again praise him,
my help and my God.

Psalm 42:5–6

As you know, O God, I get downhearted sometimes. Things start going badly, and of course my spirits sag. I love the fact that you remain with me in these troubled times. You've also felt sorrow yourself. I feel that you truly grasp what I'm going through, and that's a comfort to me. This gives me hope, and I know you'll be right beside me.

# MARCH 4

Before I was humbled I went astray,
but now I keep your word.

Psalm 119:67

It is said that a shepherd will break the leg of a sheep that consistently exposes itself to danger by straying off. As the lamb heals from this painful remedy, it learns to depend on the shepherd, who binds up the lamb's brokenness, then carries it on his shoulders, and finally guides it into safe pastures, where the lamb walks close to him.

# MARCH 5

Yours is the day, yours also the night; you established the
luminaries and the sun. You have fixed all the bounds of the earth;
you made summer and winter.

Psalm 74:16–17

*S*ummer and winter, and springtime
          and harvest,
Sun, moon and stars in their courses above,
Join with all nature in manifold witness
To Thy great faithfulness, mercy, and love.

Great is Thy faithfulness! Great is Thy faithfulness!
Morning by morning new mercies I see;
All I have needed Thy hand hath provided—
Great is Thy faithfulness, Lord, unto me.

—Thomas O. Chisholm,
"Great Is Thy Faithfulness"

We believe in a great God,
who will never fail us or abandon us.

# MARCH 6

Be still, and know that I am God!
I am exalted among the nations,
I am exalted in the earth.

Psalm 46:10

At times when stillness is not part of my outer world, Lord, I need more than ever to answer your call to quiet my heart and mind before you. I thank you that when I do stop to regain perspective, remembering that you are God, everything else finds its proper place in light of who you are. I have come to be still right now and to exalt you as God in

my life. I thank you that I can place myself under your sovereignty and find peace in your safety, provision, and love.

Solitude is the place where we can find quality one-on-one time with God. Even when life is busy, we can lay hold of opportunities for brief times of solitude whether we're driving, showering, exercising, or doing yard work—anything that allows us to be alone for a little while.

# MARCH 7

Let all the earth fear the Lord; let all the inhabitants of
the world stand in awe of him! For he spoke, and it came to be;
he commanded, and it stood firm.

Psalm 33:8–9

*Y*ou are an awesome God! I confess I should
spend more time in awe of you. Forgive me, Lord,
if I get too chummy, treating you like a casual pal,
someone I can take for granted. Yes, you describe
yourself as a loving father with the yearnings of a
compassionate mother. You say you're a friend of
sinners like me, and I take you at your word. So
I'm not apologizing for enjoying your love. I'm
just acknowledging that you are also the awesome
Creator of the universe. Let me never forget your
amazing power. Let me never stop hailing your
extraordinary majesty. You, my God, are the King
above all kings—and still, amazingly, you love me.
Thank you.

We need a new word in English, something
between *fear* and *friendship*—a word that
captures our overwhelming awe in the
presence of a great God and his invitation
to intimacy. Perhaps that word is *worship*.

# MARCH 8

The earth is the Lord's and all that is in it,
the world, and those who live in it.

Psalm 24:1

*T*ruth on the shelf of our lives is merely ornamental, but truth applied to our lives is powerful to transform us and influence those around us. And that truth belongs only to the Lord God.

# MARCH 9

Make a joyful noise to God, all the earth;
sing the glory of his name; give to him glorious praise.

Psalm 66:1–2

*I*f you can sing, sing. If you can't carry a tune, let the Spirit carry it for you. We don't need to make a symphony to the Lord, just a joyful *noise*. So sing with all your heart.

# MARCH 10

You have kept count of my tossings; put my tears
in your bottle. Are they not in your record?

Psalm 56:8

*O*ne of the worst things about my times of grief and struggle is the feeling that no one knows and no one cares. I feel all alone in a vast wilderness. I toss and turn at night, crying myself to sleep and haunted by a sense of utter loneliness. But that's not really the case, heavenly Father. Like a parent keeping a scrapbook of a child's development, you keep a record of my struggles. You not only see my tears, but you also *save* them. I can only conclude that I am precious to you, both in my victories and in my struggles. As I go through the necessary challenges of growth, you know and you care. Thank you for being with me.

Are not two sparrows sold for a penny? Yet
not one of them will fall to the ground apart
from your Father. And even the hairs of your
head are all counted. So do not be afraid;
you are of more value than many sparrows.

—Matthew 10:29–31

# MARCH 11

I trust in you, O Lord;
I say, "You are my God."

Psalm 31:14

*I* look around at my neighbors, dear Lord, and I wonder where they're putting their trust. They work hard and earn money, trying to buy some measure of happiness. They seek security in insurance policies and alarm systems. They seem to worship cars, computers, and weekends. I'm not saying I'm any better than they are. You know how often I get swayed that way, but, Lord, I declare right now that you are my God. I want no other gods before you. You are the one I trust in— you alone.

The first of the Ten Commandments is the anchor for all the others. When God is God, and we worship no other, the rest of our life falls into place.

# MARCH 12

Guard me as the apple of the eye;
hide me in the shadow of your wings.

Psalm 17:8

How intimately you care for me, Father! I look at how big the world is and at how many things there are that can harm me. And yet, as fragile as I am, I can move among life's dangers guarded by your watchfulness and sheltered by your protective love for me. I praise you for your tenderness, for your vigilance, and for making me your own child.

# MARCH 13

You desire truth in the inward being;
therefore teach me wisdom in my secret heart.

Psalm 51:6

Truth may hurt initially when we learn it, just as a needle piercing an infected wound. But after all of the pent-up lies, pride, and pretense have been let out, there is a wonderful feeling of relief and freedom that quickly follows as we embrace the cleansing of God's loving truth.

# MARCH 14

Surely his salvation is at hand for those who fear him,
that his glory may dwell in our land.

Psalm 85:9

*A*lmighty God ... bless our land with honourable industry, sound learning, and pure manners. Save us from violence, discord, and confusion; from pride and arrogancy, and from every evil way. Defend our liberties, and fashion into one united people the multitudes brought hither out of many kindreds and tongues. Endure with the spirit of wisdom those to whom in Thy Name we entrust the authority of government, that there may be justice and peace at home, and that, through obedience to Thy law, we may show forth Thy praise among the nations of the earth. In the time of prosperity, fill our hearts with thankfulness, and in the day of trouble, suffer not our trust in Thee to fail. Amen.

—George L. Locke

We cannot earn God's favor,
but God is pleased to bless those
who seek to honor him.

# MARCH 15

Open my eyes, so that I may behold
wondrous things out of your law.

Psalm 119:18

There was a time in my life when I tried to read your Word, and it just didn't mean that much to me because I didn't understand it. But Lord, the longer I've walked with you, the more precious, meaningful, and essential the scriptures have become to me. Thank you for giving me the comprehension to perceive your truth. Please continue to open my understanding to the teachings of your Spirit—the truths written in your Word—that I may walk even more closely with you.

Just as our Lord was able and willing to restore physical eyesight to the blind as he ministered on earth, so he is able to grant spiritual sight to those who seek him.

# MARCH 16

I will give to the Lord the thanks due to his righteousness,
and sing praise to the name of the Lord, the Most High.

Psalm 7:17

Along with the psalmist, Lord, I thank you.
You have blessed my life richly, and I live each day in
gratitude. Each breath I take is a gift from you. Each
move I make stems from the power you bestow. All I
am and all I have belong to you. Accept the expressions of my heart as songs of praise, my great and
loving Lord. Let my entire life be an offering to you.

# MARCH 17

I will give thanks to the Lord with my whole heart;
I will tell of all your wonderful deeds.

Psalm 9:1

Gratitude has eyes to see the subtlest shade of
blessing, the ability to feel even the gentlest touch
of God's goodness. To the Lord God I am truly
thankful for all that he has given me and those dear
to me.

# MARCH 18

Happy are those who observe justice,
who do righteousness at all times.

Psalm 106:3

*M*y Lord, I don't always know the right thing
to do, but I try. Sometimes the injustice in my world
is simply overwhelming. I don't know where to
start. Help me treat people justly, putting aside any
prejudices I might harbor. Give me courage to point
out injustice where I see it and to speak up when

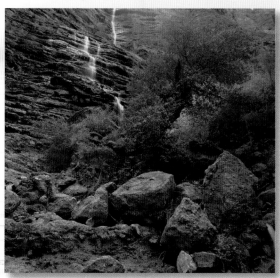

necessary, even
if that makes me
unpopular. So often
I get wrapped up in
my own concerns.
Open my eyes to see
where others aren't
getting a fair shake.

Learn to do good; seek justice,
rescue the oppressed, defend the
orphan, plead for the widow.

—Isaiah 1:17

# MARCH 19

I have not hidden your saving help within my heart,
I have spoken of your faithfulness and your salvation;
I have not concealed your steadfast love and your faithfulness.

Psalm 40:10

*D*ear Lord, when I sense that you are opening an opportunity for me to talk to someone about you—whether it's a word about your saving grace, your faithfulness, or your constant love—help me to not be afraid to speak up. Help me treat those to whom I'm speaking with gentleness and respect as I share my faith in you. And for those who are looking for you, may my words help them find you.

We can enjoy talking about our faith
if we relax and simply tell our own
story of how God has loved us so
deeply and devotedly.

# MARCH 20

Let those who are wise give heed to these things,
and consider the steadfast love of the Lord.

Psalm 107:43

*P*lease remind me, Lord, that wisdom starts with you. No matter what sort of degrees I might have, if I don't understand that your love is at the heart of all existence, then I'm missing the point. I want this wisdom to infuse every aspect of my life, and I want to share it with others.

# MARCH 21

Praise him for his mighty deeds;
praise him according to his surpassing greatness!

Psalm 150:2

*C*reating the universe. Making human beings. Speaking to Abraham and leading him. Parting the Red Sea. Giving the Law. Stopping the sun in its tracks. Burning Elijah's wet sacrifice. Taming Daniel's lions. Coming to earth as a baby. . . . These are just some of the mighty deeds I praise you for, O Lord.

# MARCH 22

He gives snow like wool; he scatters frost like ashes. He hurls down hail like crumbs—who can stand before his cold? He sends out his word, and melts them; he makes his wind blow, and the waters flow.

Psalm 147:16–18

*I*'m ready for springtime, Lord. I want to see growth and greenery, days getting longer, and breezes bringing warmth. Spring brings newness, and winter has me feeling old. But the psalmist reminds me that you are the author of both. With your creative power, you can freeze a stream and melt it. You can send a gale-force wind, and you can knit together a snowflake. I stand in wonder, awed by your amazing strength, and I ask you to work your wonders in me. Knit my life together with elegance. Melt my frozen streams of thought. Blow powerfully through all I do and say.

Though your sins are like scarlet,
they shall be like snow.

—Isaiah 1:18

# MARCH 23

Turn to me and be gracious to me,
for I am lonely and afflicted.

Psalm 25:16

*L*oving Father, you know I don't mind being alone at times, but when loneliness sets in, there's a sense of isolation and sadness that overcomes me. You made me to be a relational person, and yet sometimes you allow me to experience a famine of relationships in my life. It's at these times that I feel tremendous need for company to soothe the ache and fill the void. Please be my oasis in these times of drought. Be near me, and remind me of your presence in ways I can grasp and in ways that comfort and console me. Thank you for always being with me.

[Jesus said,] "You will leave me all alone. Yet I am not alone, for my Father is with me."

—John 16:32 (NIV)

# MARCH 24

Sing aloud to God our strength;
shout for joy to the God of Jacob.

Psalm 81:1

All of what I call "my strengths" are from you,
dear Lord. You are the source of all strength, and
I am dependent on you each day for everything.
I want to be a child who "shouts" and sings for joy
because of you, O God, my strength and provider.

# MARCH 25

Singers and dancers alike say,
"All my springs are in you."

Psalm 87:7

Dear Lord, I find myself in the season of spring,
with new life sprouting all around me. Every day
with you is like springtime, full of life and growth.
Lord, in these ways I celebrate you, singing with the
psalmist, "All my springs are in you."

# MARCH 26

O God, you are my God, I seek you,
my soul thirsts for you; my flesh faints for you,
as in a dry and weary land where there is no water.

Psalm 63:1

My Lord, where are you? You seem far away lately. Am I doing something wrong? Should I be praying differently or more often? Have I mis-

treated some friend or relative? Is that why you're so distant? Do I have a bad attitude about something? I don't know. Please let me know what the problem is so I can fix it. I long to feel your presence close to me again. Life is hard enough on its own, but I can't imagine living without you. I need to know that you're right beside me. Are you here, Lord? Please reveal yourself to me.

Be still, my soul: your best, your heavenly friend
through thorny ways leads to a joyful end.

—Katharina von Schlegel,
"Be Still, My Soul"

# MARCH 27

For me it is good to be near God;
I have made the Lord God my refuge,
to tell of all your works.

Psalm 73:28

*F*ather in Heaven! Draw our hearts to Thee, that our heart may be where our treasure must be that our thoughts may aspire to Thy kingdom where our citizenship is so that our departure when Thou shalt

call us may not be a painful separation from this world but a blissful reunion with Thee.... O Lord our God, teach us and strengthen this conviction in our hearts, that also in this life, we belong to Thee. Amen.

—Søren Kierkegaard,
"We Belong to Thee"

Knowing God intimately is to have
many stories to tell of his goodness.

# MARCH 28

Let my prayer be counted as incense before you,
and the lifting up of my hands as an evening sacrifice.

Psalm 141:2

In ancient times the sweet smell of incense would rise from the Israelites' houses of worship. Today I ask you to accept the sweetness of my praises. I love you with all that I am. I devote myself to you. I honor and glorify you. I lift my heart to you, as well as my hands. Receive my praises and enjoy their aroma. They come from a sincere heart.

# MARCH 29

Why, O Lord, do you stand far off?
Why do you hide yourself in times of trouble?

Psalm 10:1

Because you have promised to be here for me *always,* I'm going to trust you to be with me, even when you're silent. If I have sinned, Lord, please let me know. If not, then just keep guiding me, even if that guidance is subtle. And please don't stop watching over me.

# MARCH 30

O let the evil of the wicked come to an end,
but establish the righteous, you who test
the minds and hearts, O righteous God.

Psalm 7:9

*I* understand that my sense of justice is not like yours, heavenly Father. Yours is perfect, while mine is limited and skewed, lopsided in favor of myself, and I never have all the illuminating facts and information to be able to judge exactly right where others are concerned. So I'm grateful, Lord, that you know precisely how to bring wickedness to light and to deal with it. And you know how to reward what is right and true and good. Help me live uprightly,

truthfully, and honorably that I might be firmly established as one who walks in your ways, Lord.

Sir, I say that justice is truth in action.
—Benjamin Disraeli

# MARCH 31

Praise the Lord! How good it is to sing praises
to our God; for he is gracious....
He heals the brokenhearted, and binds up their wounds.

Psalm 147:1, 3

The scars you bear,
Lord Jesus, are evidence
of your wounds. You carry
them on your own body.
But let the scars in my own
life not remind me of the
wounds that made them as
much as they remind me

of your coming to heal them. Thank you for all the
gracious ways you've brought healing to my life—
to my soul, my mind, my body, and my emotions. I
wouldn't be praying this prayer if it weren't for your
healing touch. I praise you in your precious name.
Amen.

Healing this side of heaven is
a foreshadowing of the complete
healing that awaits us.

# APRIL 1

The Lord is a stronghold for the oppressed,
a stronghold in times of trouble.

Psalm 9:9

*T*oday, Lord, I feel oppressed by something or someone who seems bigger or stronger than I am or who seems indifferent to my needs or the needs of others. Please remind me not to be crushed in spirit or blinded by outrage. Instead, I ask that you would cut through my rising emotions, reminding me that you are bigger and stronger than any power in heaven or on earth. Help me lean on you and find

true comfort in you and protection from all forms of oppression.

A mighty fortress is our God,
a bulwark never failing;
Our helper He, amid the flood
Of mortal ills prevailing.

—Martin Luther,
"A Mighty Fortress Is Our God"

# APRIL 2

Rain in abundance, O God, you showered abroad; you restored your
heritage when it languished; your flock found a dwelling in it;
in your goodness, O God, you provided for the needy.

Psalm 68:9–10

*R*ain is a very good thing in the arid climate of
the Holy Land. This psalm praises the Lord for sending rain whenever the land of his people needs it.
I thank the Lord for always nourishing me with his
ever-flowing love.

# APRIL 3

Make a joyful noise to the Lord, all the earth.
Worship the Lord with gladness;
come into his presence with singing.

Psalm 100:1–2

*W*hy do we get passionately both-
ered about the styles of worship we
don't like? Worship isn't for us. It's
an offering we give to God.

# APRIL 4

O grant us help against the foe,
for human help is worthless.

Psalm 108:12

*P*eople have consistently let me down, Lord, and I'm tired of it. I feel hurt right now, and I need your help. I'm not saying I'm perfectly dependable myself; I'm only human. But my problems require a higher level of assistance. Will you bring your divine power and wisdom into my situation? Give me strength against laziness and complacency. Help me fight the temptations that pull me down. Quiet the naysayers. Calm the backbiters. Grant me the deter-  mination and confidence I need to do your work in this world.

All people are grass, their constancy
is like the flower of the field....
The grass withers, the flower fades;
but the word of our God
will stand forever.

—Isaiah 40:6, 8

# APRIL 5

I will thank you forever, because of what you have done.
In the presence of the faithful
I will proclaim your name, for it is good.

Psalm 52:9

*N*ow thank we all our God, with heart and
hand and voices,
Who wondrous things has done, in Whom this
world rejoices;
Who from our mothers' arms has blessed us on our way
With countless gifts of love, and still is ours today.

O may this bounteous God through all our life be
near us,
With ever joyful hearts and blessed peace to cheer us;
And keeps us in His grace, and guides us when
perplexed;
And free us from all ills in this world and the next!

All praise and thanks to God the Father now be given;
The Son and Him Who reigns with Them in highest
Heaven;
The one eternal God, whom earth and Heaven adore;
For thus it was, is now, and shall be evermore.

—Martin Rinkart,
"Now Thank We All Our God"

Praise the Lord with shouts of everlasting joy.

# APRIL 6

How precious is your steadfast love, O God!
All people may take refuge in the shadow of your wings.

Psalm 36:7

God's love is such that I am never disqualified from receiving it. It is always accessible to me. Only my unwillingness to accept it from him can ever deprive me of its full benefits.

# APRIL 7

Bless the Lord, O my soul,
and do not forget all his benefits.

Psalm 103:2

Today I will remember that you have given me clothes, shelter, and food. And while that list is not even close to being exhaustive, I never want to forget that you yourself are my greatest joy and my most precious gift. Help me to always remember your countless benefits. Bless the Lord, O my soul.

# APRIL 8

Worship the Lord in holy splendor;
tremble before him, all the earth.

Psalm 96:9

Today, dear Lord, I worship you with all that
I am and all that I have. Whatever creative gifts I
have, I offer them to you—songs, words, movement,
and color. You are a great God, my support and my
redeemer. You have shown me your love in countless
ways, and I love you in return. You never cease to
amaze me with your kindness and wisdom. I praise
you today, and I'll praise you tomorrow. I owe everything to you.

Before the Lord, everyone is an artist.
The worshipful expression of a God-
given imagination is beautiful to behold.

# APRIL 9

For the righteous will never be moved....
They are not afraid of evil tidings;
their hearts are firm, secure in the Lord.

Psalm 112:6–7

*F*ear might rise up temporarily in my heart, my Lord, but it can't camp there, not when I keep in mind that my future is everlastingly secure with you. Even death is not an end for me; it is the portal through which I'll pass on the way to my true

home in your presence. Anything else along my path on earth is not to be feared, because you are taking me on my journey to that eternal place of rest and delight.

Even the worst news on earth cannot eclipse the good news of the gospel, which declares God's love and saving grace.

# APRIL 10

My days are like an evening shadow; I wither away like grass.
But you, O Lord, are enthroned forever;
your name endures to all generations.

Psalm 102:11–12

reator of the universe, you make amazing sunsets. I love to watch the colors change as the light of day fades. It's truly beautiful, but it vanishes all too quickly. I want to freeze those moments in time and enjoy them longer. Frankly, there are a lot of moments I want to savor, and they all seem to pass too quickly. Life rushes on, and age keeps gaining on me. But time is nothing to you, eternal God. And the life you offer me is everlasting. I don't need to fear the tenacious tide of time. I just need to keep investing in my future life with you.

Do not ignore this one fact, beloved, that with the Lord one day is like a thousand years, and a thousand years are like one day. The Lord is not slow about his promise, as some think of slowness, but is patient with you.

—2 Peter 3:8–9

# APRIL 11

Hear my cry, O God; listen to my prayer.
From the end of the earth I call to you, when my heart is faint.
Lead me to the rock that is higher than I.

Psalm 61:1–2

*H*eavenly Father, help me approach you from a place of humility, where I can see how magnificent and strong you are—a towering rock and a powerful presence. Then my faint heart will be encouraged,

and my faith will find its rightful object. When my heart is overcome, may it be comforted when it looks up to you and helped when it calls upon you.

The Grand Canyon is an awe-inspiring place, but the lesser-known Zion National Park is, in the opinion of many, an even more powerful experience. From the rims of the Grand Canyon, one stands above the vast folds and layers and pillars of rock, looking down upon them. From within Zion, however, one enters its canyons from below and is always looking up at the towering rock features. In the same way, it's how we view God.

# APRIL 12

He put a new song in my mouth,
a song of praise to our God. Many will see and fear,
and put their trust in the Lord.

Psalm 40:3

*L*ord, please fill my heart and mind with reasons to be glad in you. I pray that these would overflow into songs of praise—songs that will continue throughout my life, lifting my own heart and encouraging others to look to you as well. In Jesus' name, I pray. Amen.

# APRIL 13

With a freewill offering I will sacrifice to you;
I will give thanks to your name, O Lord, for it is good.

Psalm 54:6

*E*very gift we give God is our heart, just wrapped up in something different each time. Our money, our service, even our praises—these are just containers for the loving gratitude of our hearts.

# APRIL 14

"Come," my heart says, "seek his face!"
Your face, Lord, do I seek.

Psalm 27:8

*W*hen I wake up, you know my first thoughts, my Lord. You know what brings a smile to my face, what makes me grumble, and what motivates me to throw the covers back and get going. But before I go to meet any of the pains or pleasures of the day, please remind me to look to you and to seek out your encouragement, counsel, and strength. How much better my days are when I take your hand and follow you through each hour! I seek your face right now and thank you for being here for me.

God is not hiding that we need to seek him. No, the problem is that we are often wandering far afield from where he waits for us. We have to leave our cities of selfishness, fairs of foolishness, and palaces of pride to find him where he is always waiting for us—in the quiet halls of prayer. We must seek him there.

# APRIL 15

Your name, O God, like your praise,
reaches to the ends of the earth.

Psalm 48:10

*M*ay you be praised wherever you are and recognized for who you are, Lord God! May my praise from this "end of the earth" rise up to meet the praises of those around the world. We give you glory and honor this day for all you have done in the past to bring about our salvation, for all you are doing even now to save others, and for all you will do to bring every promise you have made to fulfillment. In Jesus' name, I pray. Amen.

Now unto the King eternal, immortal,
invisible, the only wise God, be honour
and glory for ever and ever. Amen.

—1 Timothy 1:17 (KJV)

# APRIL 16

Blessed be the Lord,
for he has heard the sound of my pleadings.

Psalm 28:6

Thank you for hearing my prayers, dear Lord, and for being attentive to my needs and requests. Help me remember to speak often of the ways you have brought me help, deliverance, blessing, and encouragement. I want my gratitude and praise to bless you, today and always. I love you!

# APRIL 17

The heavens are telling the glory of God;
and the firmament proclaims his handiwork.

Psalm 19:1

As the changes of spring break out, my Lord (even the rains from the firmament), they shout that you exist, that you are the Creator, and that you are glorious! I revel in this onset of new life and loveliness. May I, too, be a faithful witness of who you are and what you're like.

# APRIL 18

Let them praise his name with dancing, making melody to him with tambourine and lyre. For the Lord takes pleasure in his people... let them sing for joy on their couches.

Psalm 149:3–5

*S*ometimes, my Lord, you make me feel like dancing; other times I'm just as happy to rest on the couch. In both situations, I celebrate your presence and your pleasure. I exult in the life you have given me. You created this body of mine, and I'm delighted to use it to praise you. But when this body gets weary, I can still enjoy you in the stillness. It

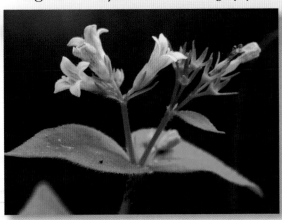

fills me with joy to think that I can give you pleasure. Be pleased, dear Lord, with my life.

Some scholars think that the psalmist's word for "couch" really refers to a mat used for kneeling, so these "couches" are dedicated places of worship. That makes sense, and it raises the question: What are we worshipping when we're on *our* couches?

# APRIL 19

With the Lord on my side I do not fear.
What can mortals do to me?

Psalm 118:6

Sometimes I let the fear of what someone thinks of me or what they might do to me wreak havoc on my peace of mind, most holy Father. You know this is so; you've seen me fret and stew about such things. I want to remember today that even though someone else might be bigger or more powerful than I am—or they might just be downright mean-spirited—whatever the case, you are greater than they are and able to shelter me from the harm

of their threats or assaults. I don't want to be afraid anymore, and with you by my side I don't need to be. Thank you, Lord.

People may harm me, even kill me, but they cannot destroy me, for God has made me his child. That is to say, through Christ, he has made me immortal.

# APRIL 20

When you are disturbed, do not sin;
ponder it on your beds, and be silent.

Psalm 4:4

*D*ear Lord, sometimes it's best to be quiet.
You've never seemed to mind it when people
express their frustrations to you. And yet, sometimes
it's best to be quiet. So let me ponder your actions,
Lord, in silence. Be with me in the stillness.

# APRIL 21

For the Lord will vindicate his people,
and have compassion on his servants.

Psalm 135:14

*T*hank you for your compassion, dear Lord.
By your compassion you have saved me from my
rebellion against you, and by your mercy you have
set me free from my sin. Thank you, Lord! I praise
your name forever.

# APRIL 22

Have mercy on me, O God, according to your steadfast love;
according to your abundant mercy blot out my transgressions.

Psalm 51:1

Depth of mercy! Can there be
Mercy still reserved for me?
Can my God His wrath forbear,
Me, the chief of sinners, spare?

I have long withstood His grace,
Long provoked Him to His face,
Would not hearken to His calls,
Grieved Him by a thousand falls.

There for me the Savior stands,
Shows His wounds and spreads His hands.
God is love! I know, I feel;
Jesus weeps and loves me still.

Now incline me to repent,
Let me now my sins lament,
Now my foul revolt deplore,
Weep, believe, and sin no more.

—Charles Wesley,
"Depth of Mercy"

The confession of evil works is the first
beginning of good works.

—Augustine of Hippo

# APRIL 23

Your steadfast love, O Lord, extends to the heavens,
your faithfulness to the clouds.

Psalm 36:5

*D*ear Lord, I rest in
your steadfast love. It often
overwhelms me how much
you love me, even when
I prove unlovable. Yet all
my limits are met by your
infinite commitment. I cannot fathom the extent of

your love. On a clear night I gaze at starlight that
began its journey thousands of years ago. Your love
out-distances that. The sun sits 93 million miles off
and gives me warmth, but your love warms me even
more. And even on a cloudy day I can imagine the
showers of blessing you're storing up for me. Thank
you so much, Lord, for your amazing love.

Spring is such a wonderful time
to enjoy the Lord!

# APRIL 24

For he satisfies the thirsty,
and the hungry he fills with good things.

Psalm 107:9

Even though my physical hunger may be satisfied and my thirst quenched, Lord, my soul still has pangs that no meal can satisfy. Only you can satisfy this hunger and thirst that nothing else is able to touch. I come to you today, hungry and thirsty for you. Amen.

# APRIL 25

This is God, our God forever and ever.
He will be our guide forever.

Psalm 48:14

In a world with global positioning systems (GPS), people rely on guidance from satellites to plot their course. After each wrong turn, the guidance is "recalculated," and a whole new set of instructions appears. This is what you do for us, Lord. You show us the way, with occasional recalculation. I rely on you to get me where I need to go.

# APRIL 26

The Lord redeems the life of his servants;
none of those who take refuge in him will be condemned.

Psalm 34:22

*W*hen I am unfaithful to you, almighty God,
when I fail to serve you well, I sometimes feel frustrated with myself and think you feel the same way.
But you don't! You simply call me back to yourself,
back to the rivers of your redemption. There I can
be washed clean, and there you can turn the tides
of my wayward self-seeking back to seeking your

kingdom and your
righteousness. Thank
you for your tireless,
redeeming love, dear
Father. I take refuge
in you today and
always.

There is therefore now no condemnation to those who are in Christ Jesus,
who do not walk according to the flesh,
but according to the Spirit.

—Romans 8:1 (NKJV)

# APRIL 27

I waited patiently for the Lord;
he inclined to me and heard my cry.

Psalm 40:1

*P*recious Lord, your Word reveals that patience is the fruit of a life lived in step with your Holy Spirit. Therefore, I ask that, instead of my trying to be patient through self-effort or beating myself up for my lack of patience, you would help me focus on being led by your Spirit in all circumstances, allowing your Spirit to guide me, speak into my life, and live through me at each juncture where patience is required. As I focus on following your lead, I know my life will begin to bear that good fruit of patient waiting and living.

The fruit of the Spirit is love, joy, peace, patience, kindness, goodness, faithfulness, gentleness, self-control; against such things there is no law.

—Galatians 5:22–23 (NASB)

# APRIL 28

He leads the humble in what is right,
and teaches the humble his way.

Psalm 25:9

Humility? Lord, I want to stay humble, to keep learning from you. Let me never assume that I know everything I need to know. Let me never claim to have attained some great level of spirituality. Whatever I am, Lord, it's your doing. I know that, and I thank you for making me the person you've made me to be.

# APRIL 29

Wait for the Lord; be strong,
and let your heart take courage; wait for the Lord!

Psalm 27:14

Dear Lord, you know that waiting doesn't suit me. But thank you for reminding me today that I don't see the whole picture as you do. Help me to not simply endure as I wait, but rather to pluck up courage and live in an attitude of faith-filled anticipation of your good plan that is unfolding in your perfect timing.

# APRIL 30

The Lord has done great things for us,
and we rejoiced.

Psalm 126:3

*I* want to take this minute, my Lord, to recite back to you as many things as I can think of that you have done for me this day, this week, this month, this past year. You *have* done great things for me! May a spirit of rejoicing rise up in me as I fill the air with testimonies of all the miracles, graces, and blessings you've poured out on my life.

Always give thanks to the Lord in the
manner you appreciate receiving God's
blessings—sincerely, thoughtfully,
and with exceeding joy.

# MAY 1

The angel of the Lord encamps
around those who fear him, and delivers them.

Psalm 34:7

*D*ear Lord, I'm humbled by all the ways you guard my life. I have seen your intervention come when I've needed it, and I know without a doubt that you are watching over me. You even send your ministering angels to bring a unique kind of watching care when I need it. Fill my heart with faith in your ability to deliver me from harm by whatever means you choose.

Angels do not seek our praise, our
worship, or our prayers. Such things
belong to the Creator.

# MAY 2

Your decrees are wonderful;
therefore my soul keeps them.
Psalm 119:129

*I* know I resist you sometimes, Lord, but I have to admit that I need your guidance. When I follow your lead, my life is far better. When I follow the teachings of your Word, I have a sense of purpose, a sense of order, and a sense of connection. You have challenged me to love others, and we both know this isn't always easy for me to do—especially with some of the "others." But when I reach out with

a kind word or do a helpful deed, the results are wonderful to behold, and things fall into place. So help me obey you more often.

If we walk in the light as he himself is in the light, we have fellowship with one another, and the blood of Jesus his Son cleanses us from all sin.

—1 John 1:7

# MAY 3

Those who know your name put their trust in you,
for you, O Lord, have not forsaken those who seek you.

Psalm 9:10

*D*ear heavenly Father, you could give me no
better comfort or assurance today than the promise that you, yourself, will remain with me. I can go
forward into any situation or encounter—into the
unknown, the dreaded, the eagerly anticipated . . .
indeed, anything!—and I know that you will go with
me through it.

# MAY 4

When I look at your heavens, the work of your fingers,
the moon and the stars that you have established;
what are human beings . . . that you care for them?

Psalm 8:3–4

*I* am in awe of the depth of your love for me,
dear Lord. You watch over my life with such care,
for you regard me as your child and crown me with
value and dignity. I am humbled and delighted all at
once. I love belonging to you and being invited into
fellowship with you.

# MAY 5

Search me, O God, and know my heart; test me and know
my thoughts. See if there is any wicked way in me,
and lead me in the way everlasting.

Psalm 139:23–24

*D*ear Lord, I want to please you inside and out.
I don't want to be like those Pharisees who prided
themselves on clean living but had greedy hearts.
I want to be motivated by your desires. Let me put away pride and even religious pride. Help me set aside self-centeredness. I want to take pleasure in your pleasure. Scour my heart so it sparkles before your holy gaze.

Woe to you, scribes and Pharisees,
hypocrites! For you clean the outside of
the cup and of the plate, but inside they
are full of greed and self-indulgence....
First clean the inside of the cup, so that
the outside also may become clean.

—Matthew 23:25–26

# MAY 6

It is you who light my lamp;
the Lord, my God, lights up my darkness.

Psalm 18:28

You really do light up my way, Lord! Whenever I feel myself groping in the darkness of uncertainty, confusion, or fear, I turn to you, and you  enlighten my mind to the truth and show me the way through. I depend on your guiding Holy Spirit and your Word to illuminate my heart and mind with truth and wisdom for making right choices. How lost I would be without you! So I look to you again today to light my way, dear Lord. Please come and light up my darkness.

On dark nights while camping in the woods, one cannot walk even ten feet without tripping over something—a root or a rock—otherwise easily stepped over in the daytime. The smallest light in such thick darkness is a great blessing. What bit of light in my darkness can I be thankful for today?

# MAY 7

I am like a green olive tree in the house of God.
I trust in the steadfast love of God forever and ever.

Psalm 52:8

*I*'ve seen trees, Lord, that are thick with age, standing tall and strong. These trees provide shelter from the rain and shade from the sun. They beautify the landscape. In all these ways, they provide joy and benefit to everyone in the vicinity. I want to be like that, too. Build me up, make me strong, and let me be a blessing to everyone around me.

# MAY 8

And now, O Lord, what do I wait for?
My hope is in you.

Psalm 39:7

*I*t's a world full of waiting, Lord. People wait for paychecks, phone calls from loved ones, and the end of the working day. What am I waiting for? Ultimately you are the only one worth waiting for. What "better life" could there be than a life spent with you?

# MAY 9

Unless the Lord builds the house, those who build it labor in vain.
Unless the Lord guards the city, the guard keeps watch in vain.

Psalm 127:1

*B*uild my life, supreme Lord, and keep watch over it. You know I have often tried to build my life in my own way. I have made my own choices about relationships, school, work, activities, and so on. Sometimes you have seen fit to bless my decisions,

but other times I just find that these parts of my life are empty, pointless, and unsatisfying. So let me now turn over the building process to you, my Lord. Guide me in all my life decisions and guard my heart.

For we are God's servants, working together;
you are God's field, God's building.

—1 Corinthians 3:9

# MAY 10

The counsel of the Lord stands forever,
the thoughts of his heart to all generations.

Psalm 33:11

*W*ho has known the mind of God? And yet, Lord, you have revealed to us a glimpse of what you are like through the counsel of your true and eternal Word. Help me search out and value the thoughts of your heart by studying the scriptures. Open my heart and mind to the wonders of your self-disclosure. May I love and search it out like a buried treasure. And may my example of loving your Word inspire a new generation to seek you out as well.

"For who has known the mind of the Lord so as to instruct him?" But we have the mind of Christ.

—1 Corinthians 2:16

# MAY 11

The Lord is my strength and my might;
he has become my salvation.

Psalm 118:14

*D*ear Lord, there's this notion that we are supposed to improve ourselves—that is, be more able to support ourselves and "carry our own weight." But I'm not convinced that my own strength is of any benefit to me. When I seem to have a lot of it, I grow independent of you; but when I feel weak, I stay close to you and am carried along by your strength.

 I'm beginning to believe my biggest strength is my weakness—that is, the realization of my great need for you.

[The Lord] said to me, "My grace is sufficient for you, for power is made perfect in weakness." So, I will boast all the more gladly of my weaknesses, so that the power of Christ may dwell in me.

—2 Corinthians 12:9

# MAY 12

By your favor, O Lord,
you . . . established me as a strong mountain.

Psalm 30:7

Is there a mountain at which you can gaze today, whether out your window or in a picture? Let it remind you of how firmly God has established your faith by his grace.

# MAY 13

Make me to know your ways, O Lord;
teach me your paths.

Psalm 25:4

Life with you is an adventure of learning, gracious Father! Help me look to each day with joyful anticipation. Fill me with a readiness to do your will and to change my ways if necessary. Being with you, walking with you, and learning from you are what make my life worthwhile. Thank you for being such a patient and gentle teacher.

# MAY 14

O sing to the Lord a new song, for he has done marvelous things.
His right hand and his holy arm have gotten him victory.

Psalm 98:1

My Lord, I can't begin to count the marvelous things you have done in my life. I look back through the blessings you have provided—timely help, important relationships, and wise guidance. There were tough times that prepared me for later challenges. There were joyous surprises that lifted my spirit. Through it all, you have taken good care of me, and I appreciate it. Let my life be a "new song" dedicated to you.

[Sing] not lolling at ease or in the indecent posture of sitting, drawling out one word after another, but all standing before God, and praising him lustily and with good courage.

—John Wesley

# MAY 15

As for me, I shall behold your face in righteousness;
when I awake I shall be satisfied, beholding your likeness.

Psalm 17:15

*D*ear Lord, in my mind's eye I see the faces of people I have loved. I think of the joy it has always brought me, just to see a smile, a tilt of the head, and a glimmer in the eye. Thank you, Lord, for these loved ones, and I pray now for their well-being. But I also wonder today about what it's like to see *your* face. I know the psalmist speaks in a meta-

phor, but it's still fun and exciting to think about. What sort of glimmer is there in your eye?

Beloved, we are God's children now;
what we will be has not yet been
revealed. What we do know is
this: when he is revealed, we will be like
him, for we will see him as he is.

—1 John 3:2

# MAY 16

Therefore let all who are faithful offer prayer to you;
at a time of distress, the rush of mighty waters
shall not reach them.

Psalm 32:6

It's one of the great blessings of belonging to you, heavenly Father, that I can remain calm and certain in a world of chaos and uncertainty. It's not that I am never touched by the ills of living in a fallen world; certainly I am! But it's that they don't carry me away into utter despair, and it's because you hold me fast.

# MAY 17

The promises of the Lord are promises that are pure,
silver refined in a furnace on the ground,
purified seven times.

Psalm 12:6

With you, dear Lord, a promise made is a promise kept. That's why there is every reason for me to trust you today—to trust that you will keep your word and carry out your good purposes for my life as I keep my focus on you. Help me be patient and faithful as I wait for the fulfillment of your pure and perfect promises.

# MAY 18

By awesome deeds you answer us with deliverance,
O God of our salvation; you are the hope of all the ends of the earth
and of the farthest seas.

Psalm 65:5

*O* God of our salvation, your most awesome deed was the sending of your Son. His incarnation as a human being restored the worth of your creation. His sacrifice for our sin won our freedom. His resurrection from the grave established your power over death. And we are the beneficiaries. Thank you, Lord, for this greatest of all gifts. I know I can never  repay you, but I offer you a song in my heart, a prayer in my soul, and the love that drives me forward each day. Blessings to you, unfathomable God.

Thanks be to God for his indescribable gift!
—2 Corinthians 9:15

# MAY 19

I stretch out my hands to you;
my soul thirsts for you like a parched land.

Psalm 143:6

*I* call to you from deepest need,
O Lord, hear my request.
I know I've sinned in word and deed,
But now I'm in distress.
Please overlook my errant ways,
And gaze at me with tender grace,
And help me fix this mess.
In you, dear Lord, I place my trust,
I've soured on self-reliance.
Your Spirit arms each one of us
To slay our taunting giants.
Your promises prove strong and true,
And I'd be nothing without you.
I pledge my full compliance.

—Martin Luther,
"Out of the Depths"

Times of need, calamity, and doubt are difficult to go through, it's true. But time and time again they drive us toward the Lord.

# MAY 20

I will instruct you and teach you the way you should go;
I will counsel you with my eye upon you.

Psalm 32:8

*T*each me, dear Lord. You are my teacher, and you always find a way to get through to me, whether I'm eager or reluctant. Thank you for your instruction. Keep showing me the way to live. Keep guiding me step by step.

# MAY 21

It is better to take refuge in the Lord
than to put confidence in mortals.

Psalm 118:8

*P*eople limp through life, each leaning upon someone else. What, then, if one should stumble and fall? They would go down like dominoes. But mark the wise who keep their eyes fixed ahead on God, who seems beyond but who actually makes them stand strong by his power within them.

# MAY 22

Happy are those whose transgression is forgiven,
whose sin is covered.

Psalm 32:1

Father in heaven! Hold not our sins up against us but hold us up against our sins, so that the thought of Thee, when it wakens, in our soul, and each time it wakens, should not remind us of what we have committed but of what Thou didst forgive, not of how we went astray but of how Thou didst save us!

—Søren Kierkegaard,
"Hold Not Our Sins"

Today I will remember to receive God's grace
in the way it is offered—as a precious gift.

# MAY 23

I say to the Lord, "You are my Lord;
I have no good apart from you."

Psalm 16:2

My Lord, you are the one who watches over me and keeps me, the one who provides for me and gives me strength for each day, the one who stays with me and leads me toward those places that will bring me peace and blessing, including heaven where I will enjoy eternal life with you. What would I do without your loving presence in my life? My heart brims over with appreciation and love whenever I consider all the goodness you've poured out into my life.

Then Jesus said to the twelve,
"Do you also want to go away?"
But Simon Peter answered Him,
"Lord, to whom shall we go?
You have the words of eternal life.
Also we have come to believe
and know that You are the Christ,
the Son of the living God."

—John 6:67–69 (NKJV)

# MAY 24

Mighty King, lover of justice, you have established equity;
you have executed justice and righteousness.

Psalm 99:4

Sovereign Lord, vindicate me when I have borne injustices, but even more importantly, remind me to speak and act in ways that are just and equitable toward others. Help me give people the same respect and right dealings I desire in my interactions with them. In that way, I can reflect your own character that loves what is just, right, and fair.

The deeds we do, the words we say,
Into still air they seem to fleet;
We count them ever past;
But they shall last—
In the dread judgment they
And we shall meet.

—John Keble,
"Early Warnings"

# MAY 25

Teach me to do your will, for you are my God.
Let your good spirit lead me on a level path.

Psalm 143:10

O gracious and holy Father, give us wisdom to perceive Thee, intelligence to understand Thee, diligence to seek Thee, patience to wait for Thee, eyes to behold Thee, a heart to meditate upon Thee, and a life to proclaim Thee. Through the power of the Spirit of Jesus Christ our Lord. Amen.

—Attributed to Benedict of Nursia

# MAY 26

I give you thanks, O Lord, with my whole heart . . . for your steadfast love and your faithfulness; for you have exalted your name and your word above everything.

Psalm 138:1–2

I praise you, almighty God. You are the Creator and Maker of all that is good and holy. I exalt your name and bow before your majesty. Your love for me is indeed wonderful, and your words to me are indeed glorious. I sing your praises with this humble prayer now and forever. Amen.

# MAY 27

For the word of the Lord is upright,
and all his work is done in faithfulness.

Psalm 33:4

*D*ear Lord, thank you for your Word and your work in my life. Your Word has kept me from straying far from you and has encouraged and renewed my faith again and again. And your work of grace

continues to transform me within. Day by day, you are as faithful as the sunrise. How good you are!

Scripture says that though people fall,
God's Word will remain firm and never fall.
Anyone who falls will be able to stand up
again on the strength of God's Word.

—Martin Luther,
*Faith Alone: A Daily Devotional*

# MAY 28

God is our refuge and strength, a very present help in trouble.
Therefore we will not fear, though the earth should change.

Psalm 46:1–2

*I*t's hard to keep up with earth's changes, dear Lord. Maybe the psalmist was thinking about storms and seasons, but I'm dealing with technology, social trends, and the environment. Things are spinning so quickly that I find myself growing fearful at times. But I cling to this promise, and I cling to *you*. You are, indeed, "very present." No matter what's hap-

pening in the world, you are with me, beside me, and inside me. I treasure your companionship. Please calm my fears and embolden me to meet the challenges of life with your love and power.

Look for God, and he will find you.

# MAY 29

For you bless the righteous, O Lord;
you cover them with favor as with a shield.

Psalm 5:12

These exquisite robes of righteousness God has provided for us are priceless. They fit perfectly, and they are gifts of grace meant to be worn daily and best accessorized with our sincere joy and gratitude. We are much blessed!

# MAY 30

He reached down from on high, he took me;
he drew me out of mighty waters.

Psalm 18:16

Dear Lord, as you know, I've had some difficult times. On a number of occasions in my life I have felt totally lost. But as I think back over those times, my heart is filled with gratitude, because I cried out to you and you helped me. You transformed some of those situations, but you also transformed me. So I thank you from the core of who I am today.

# MAY 31

You who live in the shelter of the Most High, who abide
in the shadow of the Almighty, will say to the Lord,
"My refuge and my fortress; my God, in whom I trust."

Psalm 91:1–2

May God the Father bless us, may Christ take care of us, the Holy Ghost enlighten us all the days of our life. The Lord be our defender and keeper of body and soul, both now and for ever, to the ages of ages.

Shelter and shade were crucial consider-
ations in ancient Palestine. The sun beat
down intensely, and at times a wind
blew in from Arabia like a blast furnace.
Maybe today we need protection from
reckless drivers and Internet scams,
but the Lord protects as he always has.

# JUNE 1

Blessed be the Lord,
for he has wondrously shown his steadfast love to me
when I was beset as a city under siege.

Psalm 31:21

*S*upreme Creator, I know that feeling, being "under siege." It's as if everything suddenly goes against me. People who were the best of friends suddenly turn snippy. Activities I once enjoyed become arduous. But, Lord, you have continued to love me, and I thank you for your reassurance in those difficult periods. Now I ask you to help me keep an eye out for others who are feeling that way. Give me a

sensitive heart to recognize the needs of those around me. Give me the courage to reach out and help.

He is the source of every mercy and the God who comforts us. He comforts us in all our troubles so that we can comfort others. When others are troubled, we will be able to give them the same comfort God has given us.

—2 Corinthians 1:3–4 (NLT)

# JUNE 2

For with you is the fountain of life;
in your light we see light.

Psalm 36:9

$\mathcal{L}$ord of life,
I drink from your fountain.
Live your life through me. I
rejoice in the power of resurrection and in the promise
of new life. Because you have
conquered death, we have
an eternal existence with you to anticipate. My soul
thrills with this great news. Let my life radiate with
your life. In everything I do, let me express my love
for you, and help me show your love to others.

All things came into being through him, and
without him not one thing came into being.
What has come into being in him was life,
and the life was the light of all people.

—John 1:3–4

# JUNE 3

Who shall ascend the hill of the Lord? . . .
Those who have clean hands and pure hearts,
who do not lift up their souls to what is false.

Psalm 24:3–4

Examine my heart today, O God! I want to draw near to you. Open my eyes to those things in me that are false and that get in the way of our fellowship. Please give me the courage to abandon any lies to which I may be clinging. Please help me walk fully in the freedom of your right and true ways.

# JUNE 4

Let the nations be glad and sing for joy,
for you judge the peoples with equity
and guide the nations upon earth.

Psalm 67:4

Dear Lord, I'm grateful to live among those who have enjoyed a heritage of knowing your Word, of hearing your gospel, and of acknowledging you as God. Times may be changing, but I ask that you would cause my heart to remain steadfastly devoted to you.

# JUNE 5

The Lord sits enthroned over the flood; the Lord sits enthroned as king forever. May the Lord give strength to his people! May the Lord bless his people with peace!

Psalm 29:10–11

*Y*ou are my King, O Lord. Blessed be your name. I magnify you, telling of your greatness. You rule the earth with your loving power. You dwell in your people and whisper words of peace and guidance. You are immense and intimate at the same

time, the Creator of all, yet friend to the needy. I will praise you as long as I live.

God is an infinite circle
whose center is everywhere
and whose circumference is nowhere.

—Augustine of Hippo

# JUNE 6

Great is our Lord, and abundant in power;
his understanding is beyond measure.

Psalm 147:5

Almighty God, when I watch a quality TV show or movie, I marvel at the way the writer weaves everything together. The character faces some problem at the beginning that turns out to be a benefit in the end. The plot unfolds perfectly so that the final resolution is surprising, yet somehow obvious. Sometimes my life is like that too, only you are the author. I'm amazed at your understanding and the way you take different elements of my character, good and bad, and weave them into something eternally valuable. Struggles of my past lead to victories in my future. It's hard to keep up with you moment by moment, but every so often I look back and cry out, "Wow!"

O the depth of the riches and
wisdom and knowledge of God! How
unsearchable are his judgments and
how inscrutable his ways!

—Romans 11:33

# JUNE 7

May you be blessed by the Lord,
who made heaven and earth.

Psalm 115:15

My Lord, you made heaven and earth. You do all things well. Every blessing from your hand is a good and perfect gift. Help me hold in gratitude what you give me today, and may I be ready to share the bounty of your blessings with those around me. In the name of your precious Son, I pray. Amen.

# JUNE 8

Be glad in the Lord and rejoice, O righteous,
and shout for joy, all you upright in heart.

Psalm 32:11

I know it's true that different people worship in different ways, my Lord. What you look for in our worship—however it is expressed—is that we worship "in spirit and in truth." It's wonderful, though, to read this invitation in the psalms to express our joy in you with literal shouts of rejoicing. I pray that you will make my joy in you overflow today.

# JUNE 9

He alone is my rock and my salvation,
my fortress; I shall not be shaken.

Psalm 62:6

*D*ear Father, please reveal truth to me. Do I have other crumbly rocks or false fortresses I look to for help, protection, or comfort? Do I look to them first and then to you as a last resort? I don't want this kind of arrangement in my life anymore. Please lead me away from them; show me how fragile and shakable they are. You are my rock that cannot be shaken. I need only you!

Where we find addiction in our lives is a good indicator of false fortresses and crumbling rocks we've set up as a form of "salvation." Seek God for a path out of addiction, whether it be to television, food, sex, alcohol, drugs, work, shopping—anything we turn to compulsively for comfort and help.

# JUNE 10

How weighty to me are your thoughts, O God! How vast is the sum of them! I try to count them—they are more than the sand; I come to the end—I am still with you.

Psalm 139:17–18

*J*ust when I think I have you figured out, almighty God, you surprise me. I keep trying to define you, to identify your systems of behavior, and to box you in—but you break out of all those boxes. I have to throw my hands up and admit that you are beyond my comprehension. And I wouldn't have it any other way. Indeed, you are overwhelmingly merciful. You have awesome power and sweet tenderness. You thunder and whisper. Your truth includes both the complex equation of the scientist and the simple song of a child. I kneel in wonder before you.

For as the heavens are higher than the earth, so are my ways higher than your ways and my thoughts than your thoughts.

—Isaiah 55:9

# JUNE 11

Let the words of my mouth and the meditation
of my heart be acceptable to you,
O Lord, my rock and my redeemer.

Psalm 19:14

*H*eavenly Father, I pray you will draw my thoughts to what is noble, true, encouraging, and loving. Please keep me from nursing hurts and grudges, keeping records of wrongs, and harboring criticisms against others. Set me free from such destructive ways. And may my thoughts, words, attitudes, and actions please you.

# JUNE 12

Sing to God, sing praises to his name; lift up a song to him
who rides upon the clouds—his name is the Lord—
be exultant before him.

Psalm 68:4

*D*ear Lord, today I lift up my heart and voice to praise you. You are a great God. You see, my days aren't always bright and sunny. There are frequent "clouds" of disappointment and struggle. Yet I find that in these times when I need you most, you ride in to help me. You are the Lord not only in the sunshine but also on cloudy days.

# JUNE 13

Truly the eye of the Lord is on those who fear him,
on those who hope in his steadfast love.

Psalm 33:18

*W*hen I think of you having your eye on me,
I picture a stern teacher warning some misbehaving child. But that's not really the right picture, is it, Lord? Maybe you are more like the mother who watches her child playing in the park. She lets the child play, but she's always mindful of her child. If her child skins a knee or is in danger, Mom swoops in to help. In the same way, your eye is on me, heavenly Father, and I thank you. Then again I think of a loving couple having dinner together. The food hardly gets touched because their eyes are on each other. Could that be the relationship that you and I have—my gaze riveted on you, and your eyes enjoying me?

Then the Lord said, "I have observed the misery of my people who are in Egypt; I have heard their cry on account of their taskmasters. Indeed, I know their sufferings."

—Exodus 3:7

# JUNE 14

Let me hear what God the Lord will speak,
for he will speak peace to his people,
to his faithful, to those who turn to him in their hearts.

Psalm 85:8

*L*ord, teach me to listen. The times are noisy and my ears are weary with the thousand raucous sounds which continuously assault them.... Let me

hear Thee speaking in my heart. Let me get used to the sound of Thy Voice, that its tones may be familiar when the sounds of earth die away and the only sound will be the music of Thy speaking Voice. Amen.

—A. W. Tozer,
*The Pursuit of God*

If I should stop to listen to God for one minute in each waking hour of the day, I would be devoting 16 minutes a day to hearing the voice of God. Is there a quarter-hour block of time in my day I could devote to listening to God, even if on some days he chooses to sit with me in silence?

# JUNE 15

O fear the Lord, you his holy ones,
for those who fear him have no want.

Psalm 34:9

*I* understand that by "fearing," dear Lord, you don't mean cowering or abject terror. You mean a proper respect, honor, and reverence for who you are that cause me to fervently desire to obey you and stay in right relationship with you. Help me regard you as I ought—to honor you well, because I love you so much.

# JUNE 16

So teach us to count our days
that we may gain a wise heart.

Psalm 90:12

*My* Lord, my days on earth have a number. That number is unknown to me or to anyone else but you. What I do know, however, is that I have this moment in which I can seek you, seek to know you, and seek to walk in your wisdom. Please help me to go about my days purposefully, yet with a joyful spirit, as I entrust myself to you.

# JUNE 17

For who is God except the Lord? And who is a rock besides
our God?—the God who girded me with strength,
and made my way safe.

Psalm 18:31–32

*M*y gracious God! You know I look to no false
god of this world—not to money or material things,
not to prestige or power, not to intellect or skill—to
sustain my well-being and happiness. All of these
earthly things can disappear in an instant from the
landscape of my life. History clearly reveals that
life's amenities can be here one day and gone the

next. Not so with
you, Lord. You are
rock steady, eternal,
and unfailing. You
alone, Lord, can
keep me safe.

The true man trusts in a strength which
is not his, and which he does not feel,
does not even always desire.

—George MacDonald,
*Unspoken Sermons*

# JUNE 18

But I, O Lord, cry out to you;
in the morning my prayer comes before you.

Psalm 88:13

When I wake up with my needs standing before me, Lord, standing right where I left them when I fell asleep, let prayer be my first response. As I lift my soul to you right now, let me continue to lift it all day long. From the time my alarm clock sounds to get up to the time I set it again at bedtime, may my prayers rise up to you as though in a continual conversation with a beloved friend, for that is what

you have called me— your beloved and your friend. My love returns to you today as I seek you and consult you in all things.

Our spiritual need to pray is comparable to our physical need to breathe.

# JUNE 19

The young lions suffer want and hunger,
but those who seek the Lord lack no good thing.

Psalm 34:10

*W*onderful Father, help me not turn an envious
eye to those around me who have strength, beauty,
success, riches...or any of those "powers" the world
values so much. No, Lord, I won't look to those
earthbound things for significance, worth, value,
or strength. I will seek you and look only to you for
everything I need.

# JUNE 20

O Lord, I love the house in which you dwell,
and the place where your glory abides.

Psalm 26:8

*T*he New Testament announces that my body
is a temple of the Holy Spirit. Your glory abides in
me! I'll savor the time spent in your presence with
the community of faith, but I also love the hours we
share together, you and I, when you whisper that
you are close beside, and even *inside,* me.

# JUNE 21

The eyes of the Lord are on the righteous,
and his ears are open to their cry.

Psalm 34:15

*W*hat a comfort to realize that you, dear Lord, always have your eyes and ears open, not just in a general way, but specifically to watch over me and to listen for my cries! There have been times in my life when I thought of you as being indifferent toward me. There have been times when I've even thought you were rejecting me. But I realize now how wrong I was—that it was just my limited perspective leading me to those wrong conclusions. I rejoice today in your attentiveness toward me, and in faith I will look to you and call out to you throughout this day and every day.

The God who is attentive to every detail of our lives—even down to the trivial, such as knowing the number of hairs on our heads at any given moment—will not fail to give his loving attention to the things that most deeply concern us.

# JUNE 22

Cast your burden on the Lord, and he will sustain you;
he will never permit the righteous to be moved.

Psalm 55:22

When I try to carry my burdens on my own,
Lord, the weight of them eventually crushes me.
In time, I become incapacitated while I stumble
along—pride-driven, stubborn, and thinking I

should be able to do this or
that. How much easier and
how much better for me to
unburden my heart, mind,
soul, and strength to you,
lifting my pack of problems
from my shoulders and
casting them onto yours!

I cannot know God's sustaining grace until
I put an end to my self-sustaining ways.

# JUNE 23

Make a joyful noise to the Lord, all the earth; . . .
Let the floods clap their hands; let the hills sing together for joy
at the presence of the Lord, for he is coming to judge the earth.

Psalm 98:4, 8–9

Let me add my voice to the praisefest, Lord Jesus. If the seas and mountains can clap and sing, why shouldn't I? Along with all creation, I rejoice in your presence. You came to our world to redeem us, to vanquish sin and death, and to restore us with the Creator. And so our response is truly joyful. This is good news, and it inspires an exultant song, today.

# JUNE 24

People go out to their work
and to their labor until the evening.

Psalm 104:23

Heavenly Father, as grateful as I am for the work you've given me to do, I confess that I grow weary of the long days and the unpleasant parts of my job. So please show me how these parts of my day can become opportunities to become more like your Son. May I learn from his example, knowing that you are working something good in me.

# JUNE 25

Nevertheless I am continually with you;
you hold my right hand. You guide me with your counsel,
and afterward you will receive me with honor.

Psalm 73:23–24

*I* went to sleep last night with you reminding me of your love, dear Lord. I awoke this morning knowing you were with me. Your presence is my comfort at all times and in all things. To know that I never will be parted from you is my greatest gift in life.

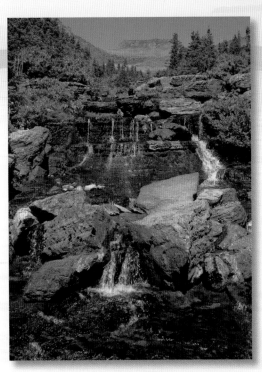

Nothing—not anything—can separate
us from the Lord, our God.

# JUNE 26

I delight to do your will, O my God;
your law is within my heart.

Psalm 40:8

$\mathcal{D}$ear God, I'm learning that life is better when I follow your lead. It might not always seem as if that's true. Sometimes I try to test out my own plans, but invariably it becomes apparent that you know better. I'm learning to seek your will from the start and not as an afterthought. In all sorts of situations, I'm learning to question my own (frequently selfish) motives and to consider what you want. Please be patient with me. I'm learning slowly, but I am learning.

Our wills are ours, we know not how;
Our wills are ours, to make them Thine.

—Alfred Lord Tennyson,
"In Memoriam"

# JUNE 27

Lead me in your truth, and teach me, for you are the God
of my salvation; for you I wait all day long.

Psalm 25:5

*S*ometimes you seem silent when I'm begging
for answers, Lord. Sometimes your silence seems
like absence, but I know you are here. I'll learn to
wait patiently and appreciate the peace of your presence, knowing that you hold the past, present, and
future in your hands. The truth is that I don't really
need answers, Lord. I need you.

# JUNE 28

All the paths of the Lord are steadfast love and faithfulness,
for those who keep his covenant and his decrees.

Psalm 25:10

*W*hat should I do, gracious Lord? What choice
should I make? So often I find myself at a fork in the
road, and I have no clue which option is best. I try
to foresee the outcome. I try to gauge my priorities.
Nevertheless, the promise I hear from today's psalm
is that your steadfast love operates in "all the paths."
Whichever road I choose, you are faithful.

# JUNE 29

I will exult and rejoice in your steadfast love,
because you have seen my affliction;
you have taken heed of my adversities.

Psalm 31:7

My Lord, sometimes I feel all alone, as if no one really knows what I'm going through or no one cares. Yes, there are people in my life, and some of them treat me nicely, but there are times when even their kindnesses aren't enough. I feel isolated, abandoned, up against overwhelming obstacles with little or no support. But a psalm like this one gets me grounded again. You have seen my affliction. You understand my adversity. In your divine knowledge, you know exactly what's going on, and you promise me your steadfast love. Even before anything changes, it's a comfort to know that *you* know. It's a blessing to sense your presence beside me. I ask for your strength now to overcome any obstacle.

Of all the great things God does for us, one of the greatest is that he *sees* us in our need.

144

# JUNE 30

I will never forget your precepts,
for by them you have given me life.

Psalm 119:93

My own ways and the ways of the world have brought grief into my life and into the lives of people I love, heavenly Father. To follow such ways is to die a slow spiritual death. Thank you for intervening in my life and for putting my feet on your path. I don't know where I'd be today if you hadn't rescued me; I don't want to imagine it. I just want to continue following you. Keep me, I pray, in your life-giving ways all my days.

A precept is a command or a principle for living life. God's precepts are intended for us to live righteously and selflessly.

# JULY 1

Happy is everyone who fears the Lord, who walks in his ways.
You shall eat the fruit of the labor of your hands;
you shall be happy, and it shall go well with you.

Psalm 128:1–2

Thank you for meaningful, enjoyable work, eternal Father. Thank you for work that provides for the needs I have. Thank you for work that helps others. Thank you for work that contributes to the well-being of society. Thank you that, in all kinds of circumstances, I can work joyfully as unto you and bring honor to your name. Let your blessings be on all the work I do, and may diligence, excellence, and productivity mark the work of my hands. For your glory, I pray. Amen.

On the heels of a job well done come the blessings of a lingering sense of satisfaction and a good night's sleep.

# JULY 2

Who can utter the mighty doings of the Lord,
or declare all his praise?

Psalm 106:2

My Lord, there are not enough words in my vocabulary to praise you as you deserve. Simple phrases like "awesome God" and "wonderful Savior" seem entirely too easy, but I'll use those, and I'll make up other praises. Yet, even more than that, I will *live out* my praises. I will seek, today and every day, to live in a way that brings pleasure to you.

# JULY 3

I sought the Lord, and he answered me, and delivered me from all my fears. Look to him, and be radiant; so your faces shall never be ashamed.

Psalm 34:4–5

The world can be a scary place, heavenly Father. With terrorism, disease, and economic uncertainty, there's not much we can count on anymore. Except you. Fill me with faith. Help me trust you for true security. Let my life radiate with confidence in your love and power.

# JULY 4

Happy is the nation whose God is the Lord,
the people whom he has chosen as his heritage.

Psalm 33:12

*T*hank you for blessing my life through your sovereign purposes for this nation in which I live. Remind me today, heavenly Father, that the values of justice, righteousness, and equity originate with you and will be ultimately and finally established by you one day. So please help me live in the light of them now, walking justly and uprightly while seeking mercy for those who are in need of it. And I pray you will guide

this nation, along with the other nations of earth, to seek you out and serve you with reverence and gratitude.

O beautiful for spacious skies,
For amber waves of grain,
For purple mountain majesties
Above the fruited plain!

America! America!
God shed His grace on thee,
And crown thy good with brotherhood
From sea to shining sea!

—Katherine L. Bates,
"America the Beautiful"

# JULY 5

You prepare a table before me in the presence of
my enemies; you anoint my head with oil;
my cup overflows.

Psalm 23:5

As I read these familiar words from David's cherished psalm, Lord Jesus, I reflect on the Last Supper, where you did "prepare a table" before your disciples. I also know that although you were about to meet your enemies, you celebrated this moment with your disciples, sharing your wisdom, your new instructions, and yourself with them. The bread and wine took on a whole new meaning, which we still observe today. Lord, thank you for the gift of yourself—shared with your disciples then and always at that table and wherever we now meet to partake of you.

For where two or three are gathered in
my name, I am there among them.

—Matthew 18:20

# JULY 6

Not to us, O Lord, not to us, but to your name give glory,
for the sake of your steadfast love and your faithfulness.

Psalm 115:1

All that I have, all that I am, I lay it down at your feet, dear Lord. All my victories, all my accomplishments, I owe them all to you. Receive the glory for whatever good things have been done through me. Receive eternal praise for the way you have molded this lump of clay, which is me. And please receive my undying thanks.

# JULY 7

For the Lord is righteous, he loves righteous deeds;
the upright shall behold his face.

Psalm 11:7

The promise of being face to face with you one day, dear Lord, is something I hold tightly to in this life. I cannot wait for the day when what I have faith in becomes visible. I want to behold the one who fashioned me in my mother's womb, who saved me with his own life, and who has cared for me by his great love. I want to see you and embrace you.

# JULY 8

O Lord, you will hear the desire of the meek;
you will strengthen their heart, you will incline your ear
to do justice for the orphan and the oppressed.

Psalm 10:17–18

*Y*ou said, Lord Jesus, in your Sermon on the Mount that the meek—the humble and lowly—will inherit the earth. This promise you've made assures me that you see how the world's system works, that you are not indifferent to the way power often becomes corrupt and abusive, and that you have a plan to set things right. Thank you that you wield your ultimate power in a way that defends the weak and needy and protects the poor and helpless. Help me reflect your heart today by standing with those whose hearts need strengthening and by standing up for those who are longing for justice.

Humility is the one posture our souls can take that leaves our hands free to give and receive God's gifts of grace.

# JULY 9

May God be gracious to us and bless us
and make his face to shine upon us.

Psalm 67:1

*W*hen your blessings flow into my life, dear Lord, it certainly feels like situational sunshine, as if you are looking upon my life with a megawatt smile. Help me remember your blessings and recount them often so that I do not forget that I have been—and always am—sustained solely by your grace. In Jesus' name, I pray. Amen.

The Lord bless you and keep you;
the Lord make his face to shine upon
you, and be gracious to you;
the Lord lift up his countenance
upon you, and give you peace.

—Numbers 6:24–26

# JULY 10

My soul clings to you;
your right hand upholds me.

Psalm 63:8

*L*ike a burr to wool, like plastic wrap to a glass bowl, like a static electricity–charged sock to polyester, like a fullback to the football, like road tar to my car's fender... may I cling tenaciously to you, O Lord. And may I feel your presence as I hold fast to you. How I always need you!

# JULY 11

Great are the works of the Lord,
studied by all who delight in them.

Psalm 111:2

*I* study my own hand, dear Lord—how it moves, the way the joints are placed, and the way my fingers and thumb work together. How amazing the design! How wise you are! Thank you for revealing your greatness in so many ways—both to the casual observer and the scholar. We all delight in your knowledge, insight, and power.

# JULY 12

I wash my hands in innocence, and go around your altar,
O Lord, singing aloud a song of thanksgiving,
and telling all your wondrous deeds.

Psalm 26:6–7

My Lord, it is a great feeling to bask in your presence. There have been times when I have come to you wracked with guilt or weighed down with worry, but you have assured me that my sin is forgiven and that you will care for me. So the burden is off my back. I am free and clear. I feel like singing.

I lift up my soul to worship you in a wholehearted expression of praise and love, and I will share your greatness with anyone who will listen. You are an awesome God!

These verses from Psalm 26 obviously refer to a range of worship activities, possibly by priests or Levites—the ritual washing, the offering of sacrifices, and singing and proclaiming. We can all understand the joy of entering worship with a pure heart and declaring our love for the Lord.

# JULY 13

For as the heavens are high above the earth,
so great is his steadfast love toward those who fear him.

Psalm 103:11

Could we with ink the ocean fill,
And were the skies of parchment made,
Were every stalk on earth a quill,
And every man a scribe by trade,
To write the love of God above,
Would drain the ocean dry.
Nor could the scroll contain the whole,
Though stretched from sky to sky.

—Adapted from "The Love of God"
by Frederick M. Lehman,
based on the medieval Jewish poem *Haddamut,*
by cantor Meir Ben Isaac Nehorai

For I am convinced that neither death,
nor life, nor angels, nor rulers, nor
things present, nor things to come, nor
powers, nor height, nor depth, nor anything else in all creation, will be able to
separate us from the love of God
in Christ Jesus our Lord.

—Romans 8:38–39

# JULY 14

I confess my iniquity;
I am sorry for my sin.

Psalm 38:18

What can I say, Lord? I have displeased you again, and I have no good excuse. I knew what was right, and I did what was wrong. I wish I could say it will never happen again, but I can't. Lord, I am truly, deeply sorry—and I'll try to do better. I beg for your forgiveness, and I count on your strength to help me do the right thing in the future.

# JULY 15

Into your hand I commit my spirit;
you have redeemed me, O Lord, faithful God.

Psalm 31:5

This was your death-cry from the cross, Lord Jesus. You were suffering for our sins, yet you forgave your tormentors. You felt forsaken by your Father, yet you committed yourself to him in those last moments. This serves as a great example for me, not just as a way to meet death but as a way to greet life.

# JULY 16

He made my feet like the feet of a deer,
and set me secure on the heights.

Psalm 18:33

My Lord, how
easy it is to slip and
fall. One minute I'm
riding high, enjoying
the blessings of life,
and suddenly I crash to
earth. Sometimes my
own pride does me in.

Sometimes I forget about you, Lord. Sometimes, like
Peter walking on the sea, I pay more attention to the
wind and waves than to you. Is there a way to stay up
there in those "mountaintop experiences"? But it's
not really the "experience" I want to hold onto, it's
you. Please stay close to me, Lord, whether I'm feeling high or low. In the heights and in the depths,
you are the one I cling to.

The psalmist refers to the mountain deer,
whose hooves are designed to grip the
rocky terrain of Israel's mountains. That's
what our faith in Jesus should be like.

# JULY 17

When the earth totters, with all its inhabitants,
it is I who keep its pillars steady.

Psalm 75:3

*I* can almost feel the earth tottering, O God. It's good to know you keep a tight grip on those pillars. Seriously, I worry about what we've done to this planet—polluted air, tainted water, depleted ozone, and melted glaciers. I know you care about the earth

too, so I ask you to help me take good care of it. Show me how to protect your creation without worshipping it. Teach me to be a good steward of what you have given us.

We know that the whole creation has been groaning in labor pains until now; and not only the creation, but we ourselves, who have the first fruits of the Spirit, groan inwardly while we wait for adoption, the redemption of our bodies.

—Romans 8:22–23

# JULY 18

Let everything that breathes praise the Lord!
Praise the Lord!

Psalm 150:6

To see the things that live and breathe on the earth is to witness your genius, almighty Creator. What a treat to see the strange and wonderful creatures and plant life you've made! Everything that breathes praises you in its own way, Lord God. Praise the Lord, indeed!

# JULY 19

The Lord is my light and my salvation;
whom shall I fear?

Psalm 27:1

This psalm asks a rhetorical question, Lord, but I will answer it anyway: No one! I need fear no one with you leading the way in my life. Search my heart, Lord. Help me to not compromise my faith in any way. As you go before me, help me stand strong in the light of your salvation and not give an inch of ground to fear.

# JULY 20

The Lord is my shepherd, I shall not want.
Psalm 23:1

The King of Love my shepherd is,
Whose goodness faileth never.
I nothing lack if I am His,
And He is mine forever.
Where streams of living water flow,
My ransomed soul He leadeth,
And where the verdant pastures grow,
With food celestial feedeth.
Perverse and foolish oft I strayed,
But yet in love He sought me,
And on His shoulder gently laid,
And home, rejoicing, brought me.

—Henry W. Baker,
"The King of Love My Shepherd Is"

Now may the God of peace, who
brought back from the dead our Lord
Jesus, the great shepherd of the sheep,
by the blood of the eternal covenant,
make you complete in everything good
so that you may do his will.

—Hebrews 13:20–21

# JULY 21

The sacrifice acceptable to God is a broken spirit;
a broken and contrite heart, O God, you will not despise.

Psalm 51:17

*I* come to you humbly, dear Lord God, well aware of my sins. I have done things to displease you, and I have avoided doing things you wanted me to do. I have not listened to your voice enough. Instead, I often go my own rebellious way. And I bow before you now in sorrow with a broken spirit and a contrite heart. Please forgive my sins. Jesus sacrificed

himself as atonement for my sins, and I claim that sacrifice now. Wipe the record clean and restore our love, I pray.

If we confess our sins, he who is faithful and just will forgive us our sins and cleanse us from all unrighteousness.

—1 John 1:9

# JULY 22

Some take pride in chariots, and some in horses,
but our pride is in the name of the Lord our God.

Psalm 20:7

*I* see prideful people all around me, righteous Lord. The "chariots" they boast about are often sports cars. It's not horses they take pride in, but houses. They flaunt their gadgets. They preen in their high-fashion garb. These are all symbols of their power. And yes, Lord, sometimes I get caught up in that too, if not boasting about what I have, then coveting what I don't. But I now renounce all of that. You are the one who made me. You are the  one who loves me. You are the one who gives my life meaning. If I ever forget that, forgive me and remind me of the truth. I am your child, and that is all I need to boast about.

Trust in the Lord with all your heart,
and do not rely on your own insight.
In all your ways acknowledge him,
and he will make straight your paths.

—Proverbs 3:5–6

# JULY 23

All my bones shall say, "O Lord, who is like you?
You deliver the weak from those too strong for them,
the weak and needy from those who despoil them."

Psalm 35:10

When I am weak, Lord, you give me strength.
When I'm embattled, you fight for me.
When I am tired, Lord, you give me rest.
When I am anxious, you calm me.
When I am clueless, you give me light.
When I mess up, you forgive me.
When I'm defeated, you lift up my head.
You lift up my heart and lead on.

"Come to me, all you that are weary
and are carrying heavy burdens, and I
will give you rest. Take my yoke upon
you, and learn from me; for I am gentle
and humble in heart, and you will find
rest for your souls. For my yoke is easy,
and my burden is light."

—Matthew 11:28–30

# JULY 24

Your name, O Lord, endures forever,
your renown, O Lord, throughout all ages.

Psalm 135:13

*F*rom the Creation to the Judgment, you will cause your name to be exalted among all the peoples of the earth. I do not even know the names of my relatives three generations ago, but I know your name, you who revealed yourself at the dawn of time to the first man and woman. I worship you today, Great One! I'm humbled when I think of you.

# JULY 25

He makes me lie down in green pastures; he leads me
beside still waters; he restores my soul.
He leads me in right paths for his name's sake.

Psalm 23:2–3

*O* Sovereign and almighty Lord, bless all thy people, and all thy flock. Give thy peace, thy help, thy love unto us thy servants, the sheep of thy fold, that we may be united in the bond of peace and love, one body and one spirit, in one hope of our calling, in thy divine and boundless love.

—Liturgy of Mark

# JULY 26

As a deer longs for flowing streams, so my soul longs for you, O God. My soul thirsts for God, for the living God.

Psalm 42:1–2

My Lord, I can relate my own spiritual life to the imagery of this psalm. Not all the time, of course. Sometimes the living water flows freely and my cup overflows with your sweet presence. But my soul moves through arid patches too—spiritual

deserts where your blessings seem far, far away. I'm not sure why it happens like this. Whatever the cause, those are tough times, and I hope I don't have too many of them. I rely on your promise that I'll find you if I seek with all my heart. I yearn for your refreshing presence.

"Let anyone who is thirsty come to me, and let the one who believes in me drink. As the scripture has said, 'Out of the believer's heart shall flow rivers of living water.' "

—John 7:37–38

# JULY 27

Be gracious to me, O Lord, for I am languishing;
O Lord, heal me, for my bones are shaking with terror.

Psalm 6:2

Terror has been all over the news in recent years, supreme Lord, and I admit it affects me too. I find myself worrying about this world, but I'm especially anxious about the well-being of my loved ones. It's not just terrorism, Lord, but health care, finances, and aging. What's ahead for us? What will the future bring? Grace. Healing. Your loving touch. Thank you, Lord, for the surety of your active presence.

Worries are like the raging sea.
Let the Lord calm the waters around you.

# JULY 28

The Lord protects the simple;
when I was brought low, he saved me.

Psalm 116:6

*W*hen I come before you as a "simple" soul,
I have no grand gift to offer. I would love to paint
a masterpiece for you, sing the best song or hymn
of worship ever, and feed all the poor people
in my county, but I can't. I just bring myself—
undecorated, unpackaged, and un-anything—
to you.

# JULY 29

The Lord looks down from heaven on humankind
to see if there are any who are wise,
who seek after God.

Psalm 14:2

*S*eeking God and his kingdom above
all else is the wisest investment we will
ever make in this life.

# JULY 30

I was glad when they said to me,
"Let us go to the house of the Lord!"

Psalm 122:1

*T*hank you, Lord, for
    the place I can go
Reserved for the worship of you.
Thank you for people who
    gather to know
What's honest, eternal, and
    true.
Thank you for love that exudes
    from that site,
Blessing my life in all ways.
I join in the worship, I feel the delight,
I offer a heart full of praise.

Sometimes skeptics say, "The church is full of hypocrites." Well, sure, but can you think of a better place for hypocrites to be? We sin in many ways, including hypocrisy, but we keep coming back to receive grace from our God.

# JULY 31

My heart is steadfast, O God, my heart is steadfast.
I will sing and make melody. Awake, my soul!

Psalm 57:7–8

The prayer for this day is a commitment to be glad in you and to let that gladness overflow into song. I pray now for a renewed steadfastness of heart that will continue to pursue the practice of praise.

Let today be a day of song, of singing your praises because you are faithful and good to me.

If you look around and find only reasons to rejoice today, praise God for his goodness, for he is the source of every good gift. But if you look around and find only reasons to be upset today, praise God for his faithfulness, for he is upholding you in the midst of your trials.

# AUGUST 1

Teach me your way, O Lord,
that I may walk in your truth;
give me an undivided heart to revere your name.

Psalm 86:11

*M*y Lord, the things that tempt my heart away from undivided devotion to you are the things of this world that offer temporary comfort, pleasure, or a boost to my ego. It's when I turn to these things for what I need instead of to you that I put them in a place they do not belong. Please make me aware of the ways in which I am fashioning idols out of other things, whether out of your kind provisions or things

expressly forbidden. Turn my heart fully toward you so that my way may not be darkened by the deceptiveness of false ways.

If a house divided against itself cannot stand, neither can a divided heart keep to a single purpose.

# AUGUST 2

For you have delivered my soul from death,
and my feet from falling, so that I may walk before God
in the light of life.

Psalm 56:13

*L*et now the heavenly hosts of angels rejoice.

Let the living mysteries be joyfully celebrated:

And let a sacred trumpet proclaim the victory of
so great a King.

Let the earth also be filled with joy, illuminated with
such resplendent rays;

And let men know that the darkness which
overspread the whole world

Is chased away by the splendor of our eternal King.

—"Exsultet,"
an ancient Christian prayer

So if you have been raised with Christ,
seek the things that are above, where
Christ is, seated at the right hand of God.

—Colossians 3:1

# AUGUST 3

The Lord will fulfill his purpose for me.
Psalm 138:8

*F*ather in heaven, you have gently and graciously created me a certain way to fulfill the tailor-made purpose you have for my life. It is a purpose that will fulfill and bless me as well as be a blessing to others. And best of all, it brings honor to your name when people see that you're the one who has brought about such good things in my life.

# AUGUST 4

Do not remember the sins of my youth or my transgressions; according to your steadfast love remember me.
Psalm 25:7

*T*he Lord's loving kindnesses indeed never cease,
For His compassions never fail. They are new every morning;
Great is Thy faithfulness.

Lamentations 3:22–23 (NASB)

# AUGUST 5

Set a guard over my mouth, O Lord;
keep watch over the door of my lips.

Psalm 141:3

*D*ear Lord, I have many regrets: a bit of gossip, a curse, a mocking tone, a complaint, a sarcastic reply, a put-down, a cruel retort, and a cold greeting. How much damage a selfish attitude and an uncontrolled tongue can do in just a moment's time! Please forgive me, and please heal the wounds I've inflicted, and if possible, allow me to participate in that healing process. Restore the relationships I've damaged and reveal to me how I can make humble amends. Help me today, almighty God, with this new opportunity to speak well of others and kindly to them, to be an encourager and comforter, a peacemaker and a blessing. For your name's sake, I pray.

There is always time to add a word,
never to withdraw one.

—Baltasar Gracián,
*The Art of Worldly Wisdom*

# AUGUST 6

As a father has compassion for his children, so the Lord has compassion for those who fear him. For he knows how we are made; he remembers that we are dust.

Psalm 103:13–14

*S*ometimes I want to believe that I'm made of physical and moral titanium, Lord, but I'm not. My best efforts are more like wood, hay, and stubble. It's only because of your mercy and grace at work in my life that I see good spiritual fruit being produced there. Thank you that you remember (and

you remind me) I'm made of mere earthly elements, and my body will someday return to the dust. Thank you that, knowing my frailties, you are compassionate toward me. I receive your kindness with deep gratitude today.

Humility acknowledges God and opens the door for his compassion to flow into my life.

# AUGUST 7

Rescue me, O my God, from the hand of the wicked,
from the grasp of the unjust and cruel.

Psalm 71:4

*J*esus, you know what it is to be lied about, unjustly condemned, and cruelly tortured and killed at the hands of wicked people. I ask that you would hear my cry for help to be set free from the evil schemes of those who would try to harm me without cause. I look to you alone for my defense. Please rescue me! In your name, I pray. Amen.

# AUGUST 8

O Lord my God, I cried to you for help,
and you have healed me.

Psalm 30:2

*T*hank you for all the ways in which you bring healing into my life, dear Lord. My heart, soul, mind, and body find new strength in you each day. Each time I cry to you for help, I am more convinced than ever that you hear me and answer me according to what I need most.

# AUGUST 9

Those who love me, I will deliver;
I will protect those who know my name.

Psalm 91:14

Jesus, the very thought of Thee
With sweetness fills my breast,
But sweeter far Thy face to see,
And in Thy presence rest.

O hope of every contrite heart,
O joy of all the meek,
To those who fall, how kind Thou art!
How good to those who seek!

Jesus, our only joy be Thou,
As Thou our prize will be;
Jesus be Thou our glory now,
And through eternity.

—Bernard of Clairvaux,
"Jesus, the Very Thought of Thee"

Love has hands to help others. It has
feet to hasten to the poor and needy. It
has eyes to see misery and want. It has
ears to hear the sighs and sorrows of
others. This is what love looks like.

—Augustine of Hippo

# AUGUST 10

Depart from evil, and do good;
seek peace, and pursue it.
Psalm 34:14

Help me, dear Lord, to seek peace. That might mean I have to back down from a fight. It might mean I don't get my way. It might mean that I don't have to be right all the time. I don't have to win. Help me put aside my selfish goals and consider the needs of others. Give me a sense of what *you* want in every situation.

Blessed are the peacemakers, for they
will be called children of God.
—Matthew 5:9

# AUGUST 11

Create in me a clean heart, O God,
and put a new and right spirit within me.

Psalm 51:10

Every sojourn outside of this sanctuary of your presence brings me back to this prayer, gracious Father. As I come to you, I sense your holiness and can feel my need to be made clean again. Please wash me with your Word, and renew me by your Spirit. Recalibrate my conscience so that it is in line with your desires for me once again.

# AUGUST 12

The meek shall inherit the land,
and delight themselves in abundant prosperity.

Psalm 37:11

Meekness is amazingly powerful, Lord! In your "economy" everything is upside down from how many people see things. You tell me to lay down everything and be humble, and you will bring your power to bear in my life to give me the best kind of spiritual life. Today, I choose your way over the world's.

# AUGUST 13

The Lord loves those who hate evil;
he guards the lives of his faithful;
he rescues them from the hand of the wicked.

Psalm 97:10

The presence of evil in the world, Lord, is often used as an argument against your existence, but your Word tells me that while evil plagues  humanity as a result of our wrong choices, you remain thoroughly good. I know you promise to establish good once and for all at the end of time, but for now, as evil and good coexist on earth, help me embrace that which is good, while turning away from what is evil. Today, as you call me to walk in your righteousness, may I respond with a willing heart. By your grace, I pray. Amen.

Those who belong to God share his delight
in what is good, his disdain for what is
wicked, and his love for all people.

# AUGUST 14

I wait for the Lord, my soul waits,
and in his word I hope.

Psalm 130:5

The promises in your Word, Lord, are the promises I cling to. Sometimes when I hear the often-quoted ones, however, my familiarity puts me in danger of seeing them as clichés. O God, forgive me for the times I've done this! May your promises always be precious to me and my hope in them remain alive. Help me to not brush past the truth

but to wonder at your Word, no matter how many times I hear or read it.

Scripture is never irrelevant to our lives, and there is always something new to discover. It only takes slowing down, pausing to look, and waiting to see. Then, in that humble expectation, we are shown what we never saw before, though we'd passed that way a thousand times before.

# AUGUST 15

Be still before the Lord, and wait patiently for him;
do not fret over those who prosper in their way,
over those who carry out evil devices.

Psalm 37:7

Why is it that those who do the right thing so often seem to lose out, while those who take short-cuts, cheat, steal, lie seem to have the advantage? Nevertheless, you call me to be still, Lord—to be still in mind and body—and to wait for you. Please take the grudging attitude from my obedience and help me wait willingly, expectantly, and patiently.

# AUGUST 16

It is well with those who deal generously and lend,
who conduct their affairs with justice.

Psalm 112:5

The presence of a gracious soul is like a heaven-sent breeze blowing through a stale room, bringing refreshment and the reminder that there are things in life far superior to one's own interests.

# AUGUST 17

You forgave the iniquity of your people;
you pardoned all their sin.

Psalm 85:2

*I* humbly bow before your throne,
Ashamed of things that I have done.
How could you ever look at me again?
My promises have come to naught.
I haven't lived the way I ought.
That's not a fitting way to treat a friend.
I will not dare to seek your face.
I plead for mercy, love, and grace.
Perhaps you could restore some tiny part?
You lift me up and take my hand,
With words I'll never understand,
And let forgiveness flower from your heart.

We don't earn forgiveness. We can't.
Excuses don't make us more forgivable,
but less. The only way to find forgiveness is to admit we've done wrong.

# AUGUST 18

Your word is a lamp to my feet
and a light to my path.
Psalm 119:105

*D*ear Lord, if it weren't for your Word, my attempts to find my way in life would look like a dizzy person trying to find his or her way, blindfolded. I can think of no better description. Thankfully, by your Word, I can discover your wis-

dom for navigating through life, which is so often in opposition to my natural inclinations. I'm grateful that you light my way today by what has been written.

God considers human reason, wisdom, morality, and even sunlight, for that matter, to be dark and hazy compared to his Word. God's Word is a flame that shines in the darkness.... If we use this light, then God will no longer remain hidden from us.

—Martin Luther,
*Faith Alone: A Daily Devotional*

# AUGUST 19

Happy are those whom you discipline, O Lord,
and whom you teach out of your law.

Psalm 94:12

*I*'ve never liked discipline much, heavenly
Father. But apparently your discipline should make
me "happy." How can that be? Sometimes I've won-
dered why the life of faith is excruciatingly difficult,
Lord, but I'm beginning to see that you're teaching
me through it all—and that makes me truly happy.

# AUGUST 20

The Lord is my strength and my shield; in him my heart
trusts; so I am helped, and my heart exults,
and with my song I give thanks to him.

Psalm 28:7

*I*t is in you, my Lord, that we are made holy,
righteous, and set apart for service to you. Thank
you for taking the initiative to make saints of sinners. And when I think of you delighting in me, I
delight in the thought of it. I cannot wait for the day
when we can delight in one another face to face. It
is indeed a noble distinction to belong to you.

# AUGUST 21

Turn, O Lord! How long?
Have compassion on your servants!
Psalm 90:13

*It* is oftentimes a small thing which casts me down and troubles me.... Strengthen me with heavenly fortitude, lest the old man, the miserable flesh not fully subject to the spirit, prevail and get the upper hand, against which we must fight as long as we breathe in this most wretched life.

—Thomas à Kempis,
*The Imitation of Christ*

When life seems unbearable, sometimes the best thing we can do is stop trying to bear it ourselves and cast ourselves, headlong with our circumstances, on God. This is not "escapism" or denial; it is simply faith in action.

# AUGUST 22

O Lord, you have searched me and known me.
You know when I sit down and when I rise up;
you discern my thoughts from far away.

Psalm 139:1–2

*I* know you see right through me.
It's sometimes terrifying
How honestly you view me.
But then I think, how awesome
That you completely "get" me.
Despite my sins and problems
You don't want to reject me.
No scowling, Lord, no scolding
In your thorough knowledge of me.
The wonder that's unfolding
Is the fact that you still love me.

For now we see in a mirror, dimly,
but then we will see face to face.
Now I know only in part; then
I will know fully, even as I
have been fully known.

—1 Corinthians 13:12

# AUGUST 23

Who rises up for me against the wicked?
Who stands up for me against evildoers?

Psalm 94:16

*D*ear Lord, grant me courage to stand up for what is right, true, and good, even if no one else will join me. Help me not waver or become afraid of opposition. Uphold and establish me in your Word and your ways. I am not strong, but in your strength I can do all things. For your honor and glory, not my own, I pray. Amen.

To do what is right is to side with the truth of God. And never doubt it, the truth of God will always prevail. Evil may cause setbacks and it may hamper the steady march of God's plan, but it is ultimately powerless to stop it. To do what is right is to join the winning side of the fight, though the battle will not be without pain or struggle.

—Charles R. Swindoll,
*A Life Well Lived*

# AUGUST 24

Blessed be God,
because he has not rejected my prayer
or removed his steadfast love from me.

Psalm 66:20

*E*verlasting God, I know all about rejection. Job applications. Bank loans. "Friends" who suddenly turn their backs. But you are eternally faithful, dear Lord, and I am truly grateful. You're ready to hear my prayers 24/7, and you keep showing me your love in unexpected ways. So today I bring my requests to you for the situations I care about, for

my loved ones, and for my own spiritual growth. Lord, please hear my prayers.

Ask, and it will be given you; search, and you will find; knock, and the door will be opened for you. For everyone who asks receives, and everyone who searches finds, and for everyone who knocks, the door will be opened.

—Matthew 7:7–8

# AUGUST 25

Happy are those whom you choose and bring near to live in your
courts. We shall be satisfied with the goodness
of your house, your holy temple.

Psalm 65:4

My Lord, I thank you for those people who
have devoted their lives to ministry: preachers and
teachers and nursery workers, administrators and
musicians and janitors. Today I pray for them. Help
them get past fatigue and discouragement to keep at
it. Continue to awaken your love within them for the
people they serve.

# AUGUST 26

Refrain from anger, and forsake wrath.
Do not fret—it leads only to evil.

Psalm 37:8

Heavenly Father, may I not enter into the kind
of consuming anger that eats me up inside. If there
is something I'm holding on to—some angry grudge
or annoying circumstance I keep mulling over—
help me let it go right now, put it into your hands,
and walk on, free of its wicked power. In Jesus'
name, I pray. Amen.

# AUGUST 27

I will walk with integrity of heart within my house;
I will not set before my eyes anything that is base.

Psalm 101:2–3

*I* Pray Heaven to Bestow The Best of Blessing on THIS HOUSE, and on All that shall hereafter Inhabit it. May none but Honest and Wise Men ever rule under This Roof!

—President John Adams's letter to his wife, Abigail, the day after he moved into the White House (November 2, 1800)

May we, as individuals, adopt this prayer for our own homes. For there is no house of government that can ever be as influential as our family homes are, nor can what transpires in government mansions be as important as what is modeled, taught, and "caught" within the sacred walls of our own households.

# AUGUST 28

Do not fret because of the wicked; do not be envious of
wrongdoers, for they will soon fade like the grass,
and wither like the green herb.

Psalm 37:1–2

*L*ord, it's hard not to get upset when wickedness
seems to prevail. I hear about horrors in the news;
I learn of crimes in my community; I am told of

 injustices in government;
I feel the effects of evildoers, even in my personal
life. But you say, in your
Word, that wickedness is
short-lived and that those
who insist on walking on

crooked paths will soon disappear: Here today, gone
tomorrow. Wow! That's sobering. Help me trust
your love of righteousness and justice that is able to
set things right. It's a good thing for me to hate evil,
but remind me to pray for those who have become
ensnared by it.

No man is condemned for anything he has
done: he is condemned for continuing to do
wrong. He is condemned for not coming out
of the darkness, for not coming into the light.

—George MacDonald,
*Unspoken Sermons*

# AUGUST 29

Fools say in their hearts,
"There is no God."

Psalm 14:1

Lord, sometimes it's easy for me to look out at the world and criticize people for godlessness. They're fools, aren't they? How can anyone see the glory of creation and *not* want a relationship with the Creator? But then I realize that this judgmental spirit is foolish too. In such moments, I humbly realize that you love fools, even fools like me.

# AUGUST 30

He has pity on the weak and the needy,
and saves the lives of the needy.

Psalm 72:13

Mighty Lord and Savior, I love you for your compassion. Many times in my life I have cried out to you in great need of one kind or another, and you have responded. Now I ask that you would make me sensitive to the needs of others. Most of all, give me your heart to extend your love to others.

# AUGUST 31

I have calmed and quieted my soul,
like a weaned child with its mother;
my soul is like the weaned child that is with me.

Psalm 131:2

Holding other people's babies is a treat, heavenly Father, but it's an almost universal reality that a baby is never truly at peace and rest until it is returned to its mother's arms. It's like that with your children. We venture out into the world and go about our business, as if we are handed around from this set of arms to another. It isn't until we can return to your presence—the resting place of our souls—that we feel like a child at its mother's breast—quieted, calmed, and able to truly rest.

If my soul is disquieted, restless, frustrated, and "fussy," perhaps it is time for me to be quieted in the arms of my God.

# SEPTEMBER 1

O come, let us sing to the Lord; let us make a joyful noise to the rock of our salvation! Let us come into his presence with thanksgiving; let us make a joyful noise to him with songs of praise!

Psalm 95:1–2

There are many ways I could come into your presence, Lord. I could approach you humbly, knowing that you're a holy God and I'm a sinner. I could come to you with questions. There's so much I want to learn from you. I could also enter your presence with a wish list of prayer requests, because you really care about the desires of our hearts. But today I'm following the psalmist's example, stepping before you with a heart full of thanksgiving. You have abundantly blessed me, dear Lord, and I erupt with songs of joy and praise.

There's no better attitude
Than gratitude—
Nothing outranks
Thanks.

# SEPTEMBER 2

I will bless the Lord at all times;
his praise shall continually be in my mouth.

Psalm 34:1

Praise to the Lord, the Almighty, the King of
creation!
O my soul, praise him, for He is thy health and salvation!
All ye who hear, now to His temple draw near;
Praise Him in glad adoration!

Praise to the Lord! O let all that is in me adore Him!
All that hath life and breath, come now with praises
before Him.
Let the Amen sound from His people again;
Gladly for aye we adore Him.

—Joachim Neander,
"Praise to the Lord, the Almighty"

The whole multitude of the disciples
began to praise God joyfully with a loud
voice for all the deeds of power
that they had seen.

—Luke 19:37

# SEPTEMBER 3

I call upon the Lord, who is worthy to be praised,
so I shall be saved from my enemies.

Psalm 18:3

*I* am uncomfortable referring to my antago-
nists as "enemies," Lord. The word *enemy* brings
to mind political intrigues and military battles.
But it's true that the people in my life who oppose
me or who seek to harm me behave like enemies
who have marked me as a tar-
get for their missions of ill will
and their arrows of spite. What
do I do, Lord? Since revenge is
not an option, I'm calling out
to you to defend me. Show me
how to respond in each situa-

tion, whether I should turn and walk away or stand
strong and demonstrate your strength and grace.
Meanwhile, I'll keep praising you because you're
in control: You do vindicate and are able to rescue
me, and you will not let me be overcome by my
"enemies."

A person may determine to be my
enemy, but it does not follow that I am
obligated to return the disfavor.

# SEPTEMBER 4

Trust in the Lord, and do good;
so you will live in the land, and enjoy security.

Psalm 37:3

At times, almighty God, evil seems prevalent in the world. But I know that evil will not prevail. You prevail in all things. So I'll keep my focus on you, and do what is right. I will choose to do good, entrusting my well-being and security to you.

# SEPTEMBER 5

But surely, God is my helper;
the Lord is the upholder of my life.

Psalm 54:4

When things go wrong in my life, dear Lord, help me live out this declaration. May I entrust to you all that pertains to my life, even my life itself: from broken bones to broken promises—every form of fragmentation, frustration, and pain that life in this fallen world can dish out. May I seek and know you as my helper, the upholder of my life.

# SEPTEMBER 6

Restore to me the joy of your salvation,
and sustain in me a willing spirit.

Psalm 51:12

*I* come to you with a tired soul.
My will seems weak; my faith feels old.
I've said the words, the prayers I've prayed;
Good deeds I've done; I've seldom strayed.
My interaction with you, Lord,
Is fine—but now I'm getting bored.
I trust you still for daily bread,
Just lately I've been playing dead.
But wait! Before the break of day
My tombstone slowly rolls away!
The Lord of life stands tall and strong.
I think I hear a victory song.
The risen Christ is raised indeed,
And after that, he raises me.
Salvation's joy has been restored.
Sing praises to our living Lord!

In fact Christ has been raised from the dead,
the first fruits of those who have died.

—1 Corinthians 15:20

# SEPTEMBER 7

Sing praises to the Lord with the lyre, with the lyre and the sound of melody. With trumpets and the sound of the horn make a joyful noise before the King, the Lord.

Psalm 98:5–6

*W*hat instruments do I have to praise you with, dear Lord? The whoosh of the photocopier as I do my office work? The gurgle of the coffeemaker in the kitchen? Perhaps even that annoying sound in my car engine could join in the symphony of praise.

I want to gather elements of my entire life and offer them to you. I don't stop being your child when I work, or when I drive, or when I sip a steaming cup of coffee. The music comes from every aspect of my world, and I offer it all to you as my paean of praise.

Whether at sea or on land,
Whether in the air or in your home,
Whether during calm days or stormy nights,
Whether alone or with others,
Praise our Redeemer and Lord.

# SEPTEMBER 8

You, O Lord, are a shield around me,
my glory, and the one who lifts up my head.

Psalm 3:3

Dear Lord, I thank you for these three wonderful things you do for me: First, you shield me from harm. Second, through you I connect with your amazing and eternal resplendence. Finally, you "lift up my head." When I'm in the doldrums, you come to me with exceeding joy. Thank you for these remarkable gifts.

# SEPTEMBER 9

Restore us, O Lord God of hosts;
let your face shine, that we may be saved.

Psalm 80:19

Restoration may be a process, but the way of restoration is just one step away—a single decision to leave our own path and get in step with God's Spirit.

# SEPTEMBER 10

For God alone my soul waits in silence; from him comes
my salvation. He alone is my rock and my salvation,
my fortress; I shall never be shaken.

Psalm 62:1–2

*S*ometimes, Lord, I just need to get away from it all—to be quiet and rest. Thank you for providing a place of rest. Life spins so quickly that I can't always keep up. I start to worry about what might happen. Those worries then add stress to my life, affecting the way I work and the way I relate to others. Friendships get frayed, mistakes get made, and

I have even more to worry about. So right now I'm quieting down, and I'm turning to you for help. I trust you to provide the deliverance I need.

Do not worry about anything, but in everything by prayer and supplication with
thanksgiving let your requests be made
known to God. And the peace of God, which
surpasses all understanding, will guard your
hearts and your minds in Christ Jesus.

—Philippians 4:6–7

# SEPTEMBER 11

O Lord, who may abide in your tent? Who may dwell on
your holy hill? Those who walk blamelessly, and do what is right,
and speak the truth from their heart.

Psalm 15:1–2

*I*n the little sin "allowances" I
sometimes make for myself, loving
Father—allowances to lie or cheat or
steal, even in the smallest of ways—
I undermine our fellowship and
estrange myself from being at peace
with you in your presence. There is nothing in this
world that is worth that sacrifice. Please wake me
up today to the things I am doing that are not pure
and right and true. May your Spirit bring a sense
of grief to my heart at the wrong of such things.
Then I will confess them and seek to forsake them
and be reconciled to you at once. In Jesus' name,
I pray. Amen.

Catch for us the foxes, the little
foxes that ruin the vineyards,
our vineyards that are in bloom.

—Song of Songs 2:15 (NIV)

# SEPTEMBER 12

You shall eat the fruit of the labor of your hands;
you shall be happy, and it shall go well with you.

Psalm 128:2

O my Father in heaven, I love doing your work. It's a great feeling to be filled with your strength, to use the abilities you have given me, and to accomplish something in your name. I realize that it's only through your power that I accomplish anything. To know that you are pleased with my effort—that makes it all worthwhile.

# SEPTEMBER 13

Faithfulness will spring up from the ground,
and righteousness will look down from the sky.

Psalm 85:11

When you preside over hearts, homes, and nations, Lord, your ways become established. Please make me one of those people whose presence is a pleasant place for others to be. Reveal your own goodness through my life—your righteousness and faithfulness. In your name, I ask. Amen.

# SEPTEMBER 14

Young men and women alike, old and young together!
Let them praise the name of the Lord, for his name alone is exalted;
his glory is above earth and heaven.

Psalm 148:12–13

*D*ear Lord, you know I have my ways of worshipping you. There are certain songs I like and certain actions I'm accustomed to. There's a certain style I've learned that really makes me feel close to you. But I know you're a big God, and you have a lot of worshippers. Different ages and genders, and also different cultures—everyone can bring their own styles to worship. It's not always easy for me to wor-

ship you in someone else's style, but I can try. That's what it means to be a congregation, I guess—to be a family, to be the people of God.

I will pour out my spirit on all flesh; your
sons and your daughters shall prophesy,
your old men shall dream dreams,
and your young men shall see visions.

—Joel 2:28

# SEPTEMBER 15

From your lofty abode you water the mountains;
the earth is satisfied with the fruit of your work.

Psalm 104:13

For the beauty of the earth, for the glory
of the skies,
For the love which from our birth, over and around
us lies,
Lord of all, to Thee we raise, this our hymn of
grateful praise.

For each perfect gift of Thine, to our race so freely
given,
Graces human and divine, flowers of earth and buds
of Heaven.
Lord of all, to Thee we raise, this our hymn of
grateful praise.

—Folliot S. Pierpoint,
"For the Beauty of the Earth"

As for those who in the present age
are rich, command them not to be
haughty, or to set their hopes on the
uncertainty of riches, but rather on
God who richly provides us with
everything for our enjoyment.

—1 Timothy 6:17

# SEPTEMBER 16

My times are in your hand;
deliver me from the hand of my enemies and persecutors.

Psalm 31:15

*W*hy does life get increasingly difficult, my Lord? It's hard to get out of bed in the morning. I know life has its ups and downs, but I could stand a few more ups and a lot fewer downs. Let me remember, Lord, that "my times are in your hand." You ride that roller coaster with me, don't you? Good times and bad, you have a handle on them all.

# SEPTEMBER 17

Ascribe to the Lord, O families of the peoples,
ascribe to the Lord glory and strength.

Psalm 96:7

*F*ather in heaven, you *are* glorious! More glorious than the most awe-inspiring sunrise or the wonders of the night sky. You *are* strong, Lord! Stronger than the most powerful ocean currents or the eruption of volcanic mountains. You are amazing, my God! I am full of wonder at your works and your ways. Amen.

# SEPTEMBER 18

Though an army encamp against me,
my heart shall not fear; though war rise up against me,
yet I will be confident.

Psalm 27:3

*S*ometimes it seems that I'm fighting a losing battle. Life gets difficult, Lord, and it feels as if everyone and everything is against me. I seem to say the wrong thing. People misunderstand me. My daily work is harder than it should be. Even stoplights turn red as I approach. What's going on?

Is the entire universe my enemy? Well, no, you are still on my side, and you are much bigger and more powerful than the whole rest of the universe—besides, you *made* it! When the rest of my life becomes a struggle, I can still rely on your support. Thank you, Lord.

And this is the victory that conquers
the world, our faith.

—1 John 5:4

# SEPTEMBER 19

With my mouth I will give great thanks to the Lord; I will praise him in the midst of the throng. For he stands at the right hand of the needy, to save them from those who would condemn them to death.

Psalm 109:30–31

*S*how me where to stand, gracious Lord. If you stand at the right hand of the needy, I want to be there too. What can I do to help? Soften my heart and sharpen my eyes so I notice the needs around me and feel the urge to assist. I know I can't solve

everyone's problems, but I want to reach out with your love and power to make life a little better for someone who's hurting. Please show me the way.

Has not God chosen the poor in the world to be rich in faith and to be heirs of the kingdom that he has promised to those who love him?

—James 2:5

# SEPTEMBER 20

I would feed you with the finest of the wheat,
and with honey from the rock I would satisfy you.

Psalm 81:16

*I* thank you, dear Lord, for your daily provision. Day by day, you sustain my life. Once in a while you surprise me with some unexpected blessing. The psalmist talks about "honey from the rock," and honestly the last thing I expect from my rocky existence is sweetness. I have learned to trust you for what I need each day. They make life with you a delight.

# SEPTEMBER 21

I cry to God Most High,
to God who fulfills his purpose for me.

Psalm 57:2

*You* know all the purposes for which you have made me, Lord God: to fellowship with you; to enjoy meaningful relationships with others; to declare your praises; to minister to those in need... the list is long. Yet, you are the one who fulfills your purpose for those who love you.

# SEPTEMBER 22

All the earth worships you;
they sing praises to you,
sing praises to your name.

Psalm 66:4

May I hear the songs of praise around me,
great Lord, as I, too, seek to worship you in song.
The songbirds, geese, flowing waters, ocean waves,
falling rain, thunderstorms, rustling leaves, frogs,
crickets, coyotes, wolves . . . so much of nature sings,
and to me it sounds as if praise and thanks are being
lifted to you. It sounds as if your creation is reveling

in your goodness.
Today I'll join my
voice to theirs, and
together we will
worship you.

What music can you hear right now as you
listen, whether it be music from within or
from without? Use it as a springboard for
your own worship right now!

# SEPTEMBER 23

[God] satisfies you with good as long as you live
so that your youth is renewed like the eagle's.

Psalm 103:5

*I* rise today,
Through the strength of Heaven,
Light of Sun,
Brilliance of Moon,
Splendor of Fire,
Speed of Lightning,
Swiftness of Wind,
Depth of Sea,
Stability of Earth,
Firmness of Rock.

—breastplate of Patrick

Even youths will faint and be weary,
and the young will fall exhausted;
but those who wait for the Lord
shall renew their strength, they shall
mount up with wings like eagles,
they shall run and not be weary,
they shall walk and not faint.

—Isaiah 40:30–31

# SEPTEMBER 24

Blessed be the Lord, who daily bears us up;
God is our salvation.

Psalm 68:19

When I read this verse, dear Lord, I think of a father scooping up his daughter to carry her in his arms or on his shoulders. I think of the delight on the child's face as she is raised to that place of security and fellowship. This is how you are with your children, heavenly Father. This is how you bear us up each day. My trust belongs to you.

# SEPTEMBER 25

You crown the year with your bounty.

Psalm 65:11

By your grace, heavenly Father, another harvest has been gathered in—all those grains, fruits, and vegetables to sustain our lives. My great God, help me keep a light heart, remembering your goodness and praising you for your provisions, both physical and spiritual.

# SEPTEMBER 26

Our soul waits for the Lord; he is our help and shield.
Our heart is glad in him, because we trust in his holy name.

Psalm 33:20–21

Lord Jesus, while you were on the earth, you reminded us that there would be wars and we would hear rumors of wars until your return. How we look forward to the day when you will bring your peace to fully rule over all! Until then, we find our peace in the refuge of your promises and in the comforting presence of your Holy Spirit. In you, though, we

don't just take cover until you come back again, but rather we rise up in triumphant rejoicing because we trust in you.

People will wait patiently, excitedly in line for the release of a long-awaited product when it hits the stores or a movie when it arrives at the box office. How much more should we have that attitude today as we await the Lord's promised intervention in our lives!

# SEPTEMBER 27

Lord, you have been our dwelling place
in all generations.

Psalm 90:1

You are my dwelling place, O Lord.
You are my home, my hearth,
Where I lay my head at night
And ease my heart.
I can unwind in your presence,
Set my burdens down,
With you, Lord, I'm free to be
Myself.
You are my place of nurture.
You are my place of nourishment.
You let me digest
My stress.
How good it is each day, dear Lord,
To come home to you.

Jesus answered him, "Those who love
me will keep my word, and my Father
will love them, and we will come to
them and make our home with them."

—John 14:23

# SEPTEMBER 28

The voice of the Lord is over the waters; the God of glory thunders,
the Lord, over mighty waters.

Psalm 29:3

The thunder rolls, supreme and all-powerful God, and I think of your mighty voice speaking light into darkness. The lightning flashes, and I also think of those flashes of insight you give us. Awesome Lord, I ask you to thunder into my life. Give me flashes of clarity to know how to serve you most effectively in this challenging world.

# SEPTEMBER 29

For the Lord hears the needy,
and does not despise his own that are in bonds.

Psalm 69:33

O Lord, I'm trapped! I've gotten myself in a situation I cannot get out of. This bondage is suffocating, and I feel panicked. I didn't listen to you, and now it's too late to heed the wisdom of your counsel. Please forgive me and rescue me. Have mercy on me! In Jesus' name, I pray. Amen.

# SEPTEMBER 30

I lift up my eyes to the hills—from where will my help come?
My help comes from the Lord, who made heaven and earth.

Psalm 121:1–2

*A*ll my life, Lord, I've been lifting up my eyes in various directions, hoping to find the help I need. A career path, a financial plan, popularity, home, and family. I know they're not bad things, but I tend to put them up on a pedestal and expect them to save me. How many of us were counting on savings accounts and retirement plans when the economy went south? That's a hard lesson to learn. And when those idols crumble, many of us turn to various escapes—alcohol, drugs, and so on. You know the escapes I've tried,  but I keep coming back to you. Where does my help come from? From the loving Lord who made me. I put my trust in you.

In the psalmist's time, "the hills" were where idol-worshippers had their sacred groves. Help comes, not from the hills, but from the One who *made* the hills.

# OCTOBER 1

Happy are those who do not follow the advice of the wicked . . . ;
but their delight is in the law of the Lord,
and on his law they meditate day and night.

Psalm 1:1–2

*G*od, in this psalm I see the importance of the influences I choose each day. Thank you that even this time I am spending with you right now is a safeguard for my soul. The closer I stick to you, and

the more I fill my mind with your Word, the more strength I have to do the right thing. Please keep my heart and mind free of the clutter of compromise and half-truths. Thank you for the way your Word clarifies and simplifies my life. Counsel me with your truth today and every day. In your name, I pray. Amen.

There will be many moral junctures in the course of my day today. What I truly believe will be revealed in how I navigate each one.

# OCTOBER 2

Do not be far from me,
for trouble is near
and there is no one to help.

Psalm 22:11

*W*e beseech thee, Master, to be our helper and
protector.
Save the afflicted among us;
have mercy on the lowly;
raise up the fallen;
appear to the needy;
heal the ungodly;
restore the wanderers of thy people;
feed the hungry;
ransom our prisoners;
raise up the sick;
comfort the faint-hearted.

—Clement of Rome

Remember, I am with you always,
to the end of the age.

—Matthew 28:20

# OCTOBER 3

I treasure your word in my heart,
so that I may not sin against you.
Psalm 119:11

To take in a bit of your Word each day, my supreme Lord, is to feed my soul and spirit. Even a small morsel of truth from you can be multiplied throughout my day like the loaves and the fishes were after Jesus' seaside sermon. And when I "chew" on a passage of scripture, it not only nourishes my faith but also strengthens my resistance to tempta-

tion. Thank you for the precious resource of your Word that reminds me of and keeps me safe in your will.

It has been said of the Bible:
"This book will keep me from sin,
or sin will keep me from this book."

# OCTOBER 4

The law of the Lord is perfect, reviving the soul;
the decrees of the Lord are sure, making wise the simple.

Psalm 19:7

Revive my soul, dear Lord, as I open your Word. Show me how to live. Move me into new enterprises that will serve you. Lead me into adventures in my activities and relationships. Give me the courage to try some things that have never been tried before. Overcome the barriers I put up, and let your awesome power explode through me.

# OCTOBER 5

Sing praises to the Lord, O you his faithful ones,
and give thanks to his holy name.

Psalm 30:4

My Lord, even when I don't feel like singing, please remind me of how much you deserve to be praised. Help me express my song along with the help of others who are singing your praises. Don't let me miss an opportunity to sing your praises today. You're truly deserving of every bit of worship that I can lift to you.

# OCTOBER 6

The Lord upholds all who are falling,
and raises up all who are bowed down.

Psalm 145:14

O Lord! Thou knowest how busy I must be this day: if I forget thee, do not thou forget me.

—Sir Jacob Astley

The prayer above was uttered by a soldier before a battle in the English Civil War. Some of our days on earth can be like a series of little wars on many fronts. How consumed we can become by them, by the energy and attention they require of us! If we forget God in the heat of battle, however, he does not forget us. And when we become mindful again of our need for him, he is just as near as he was the last time we were fully aware of his presence.

# OCTOBER 7

You will not fear the terror of the night, or the arrow
that flies by day, or the pestilence that stalks in darkness,
or the destruction that wastes at noonday.

Psalm 91:5–6

*O* Lord, I see terror all around me. People are
afraid to travel, afraid to invest, and afraid even to
step outside. The world is a powder keg, the economy is iffy, and I never know if I'm coming down
with the flu or some dread disease. Yet you tell me
I don't need to be afraid, and I'll take you at your
word. Whatever might happen to my world or to me,

I know that you
will be with me. I
find great comfort
in that assurance.
Give me the ability
to comfort
others with that
same truth.

Terror thrives on uncertainty.
While we may not know what
the future holds, we certainly
know who holds the future.

# OCTOBER 8

Wash me thoroughly from my iniquity,
and cleanse me from my sin.

Psalm 51:2

*O* Lord, who hast mercy upon all, take away from me my sins, and mercifully kindle in me the fire of thy Holy Spirit. Take away from me the heart of stone, and give me a heart of flesh, a heart to love and adore thee, a heart to delight in thee, to follow and to enjoy thee, for Christ's sake.

—Ambrose of Milan

# OCTOBER 9

I will praise the name of God with a song;
I will magnify him with thanksgiving.

Psalm 69:30

*H*eavenly Father, I want to recommit to singing my praises to you. I want to sing a love song to you or a hymn or maybe a worship chorus. Singing to you helps me draw near you like no other form of prayer. Thank you for the gift of music!

# OCTOBER 10

At an acceptable time, O God, in the abundance of your steadfast love, answer me. With your faithful help rescue me from sinking in the mire.

Psalm 69:13–14

*D*ear Lord, I usually track quite well with the psalmist. The details are different, but the essential situations still exist—trouble, enemies, and a need for deliverance in tough times. This particular psalm is the story of my life, too. So I have to laugh a little when the psalmist cries out for help "at an acceptable time." As I picture it, the psalmist is sinking in quicksand, about to be swallowed up, and the prayer is: "When you have a minute, Lord, if it's not too much trouble, would you think about saving me?" I laugh, but then I realize that time is often the issue. I pray for all sorts of things that I want *now,* and I complain when you don't immediately respond. Maybe, in your wisdom, you're just waiting for "an acceptable time."

God has all the time in the world, and then some.

# OCTOBER 11

O magnify the Lord with me,
and let us exalt his name together.

Psalm 34:3

$\mathcal{D}$ear Lord, I can talk with my friends about anything and everything— traffic, children, weather, TV, and sports—you name it. But it's harder to talk about you. Why is that? Lord, it should be the most natural thing in the world to share what you're doing in my life and to hear similar reports from others. Help me open up about you, so my friends and I can magnify you together.

You are the light of the world. A city built on a hill cannot be hid. No one after lighting a lamp puts it under the bushel basket, but on the lampstand, and it gives light to all in the house. In the same way, let your light shine before others.

—Matthew 5:14–16

# OCTOBER 12

Let me hear of your steadfast love in the morning, for in you
I put my trust. Teach me the way I should go,
for to you I lift up my soul.

Psalm 143:8

Lord, thou hast given us thy Word for a light to
shine upon our path; grant us so to meditate on that
Word, and to follow its teaching, that we may find
in it the light that shines more and more until the
perfect day; through Jesus Christ our Lord.

—Jerome of Stridon

# OCTOBER 13

I give thanks to you, O Lord my God, with my whole heart,
and I will glorify your name forever.

Psalm 86:12

Supreme Creator, I want to dwell on your goodness. The reality of your blessings never stops, but
when my perception of them fails, please remind me
of better times and that you are worthy of my praise
at all times. That way, I can keep on giving you the
glory you richly deserve.

# OCTOBER 14

Let the righteous be joyful;
let them exult before God;
let them be jubilant with joy.

Psalm 68:3

Great God on high, I join the angels in singing your praise. With all creation I celebrate your artistry. And along with all humans who have tasted of your mercy, I sing a song of redemption. You are more than worthy of my everlasting attention, dear Lord. You bring great joy to my heart, and now that joy is exploding back in your direction. Hallelujah, my wonderful sovereign! Hail to you, majestic ruler! Thank you, my beloved friend.

Then I heard what seemed to be the voice of a great multitude, like the sound of many waters and like the sound of mighty thunderpeals, crying out, "Hallelujah! For the Lord our God the Almighty reigns. Let us rejoice and exult and give him the glory."

—Revelation 19:6–7

# OCTOBER 15

The steadfast love of the Lord is from everlasting to everlasting
on those who fear him,
and his righteousness to children's children.

Psalm 103:17

Almighty Father, in a world where everything seems to be changing by the minute, the word "steadfast" is like a neon sign, indicating a place of refuge. And that is what your love is, Lord: a refuge, the one thing we can count on in life and the thing that doesn't change. I never know what the price of fuel will be in the morning, but I know I will wake up with the assurance of your love. May each successive generation—my children, grandchildren, great-grandchildren, and beyond—come to know the assurance of your steadfast love.

It is said that, in life, only death and taxes are certain, but what is truly certain in this life? For starters, God's love and his faithfulness. How much better are these certainties than the other supposed ones! How much better life seems in light of them!

# OCTOBER 16

I will sing of your steadfast love, O Lord, forever;
with my mouth I will proclaim your faithfulness to all generations.

Psalm 89:1

Heavenly Father, I wonder how many people are thinking of you and how good you are to them. I would be extremely happy to be able to gently and yet effectively plant a seed of your gracious love in their hearts and minds. But if all I can do is pray for them, then I'll gladly do that today with hope that you are at work within them.

# OCTOBER 17

You have multiplied, O Lord my God, your wondrous deeds
and your thoughts toward us; none can compare with you.

Psalm 40:5

Dear Lord, I thank you for every smile from someone I love. Every breath I draw and every beat of my heart. Every color in the spectrum of an evening sky or a bird's plumage. I thank you for all these things and much, much more.

# OCTOBER 18

I bless the Lord who gives me counsel; in the night also
my heart instructs me. I keep the Lord always before me;
because he is at my right hand, I shall not be moved.

Psalm 16:7–8

My Lord, I think of the various "counselors" I've had in my life. It's a mixed bag. Parents, friends, ministers, teachers, coaches, camp counselors, and guidance counselors in school. Some of them brought true wisdom, and I believe you used them to guide me in your path. Others had different motives. Some were fully invested, caring deeply about me. Others were more interested in hearing themselves talk, and they didn't hang around long enough to see the results. But you, Lord, are a counselor who cares, stays close to me, and knows me deeply. Keep counseling me, day and night, and I'll keep listening for your voice.

His Holy Spirit speaks to us deep
in our hearts and tells us that
we are God's children.

—Romans 8:16 (NLT)

# OCTOBER 19

Relieve the troubles of my heart,
and bring me out of my distress.

Psalm 25:17

While life's dark maze I tread,
And griefs around me spread,
    be Thou my Guide;
Bid darkness turn to day,
    wipe sorrow's tears away,
    Nor let me ever stray
        from Thee aside.

—Ray Palmer,
"My Faith Looks Up to Thee"

The troubles of my heart today are not too small to be insignificant to God, nor are they too big to be insurmountable for him. The mere fact that my heart is troubled draws his attention, his mercy, and his aid.

231

# OCTOBER 20

Praise the Lord! Happy are those who fear the Lord,
who greatly delight in his commandments.

Psalm 112:1

Lord, I'm trying to understand what it means to "fear" and "delight." To me, they seem completely opposite. Maybe "fear" is mainly a recognition that you pay attention to what I do. The way I live my life matters to you. Then "delight" could be the knowledge that you help me live right and that you forgive me when I don't. Help me to do both rightly!

# OCTOBER 21

Let the redeemed of the Lord say so, those he redeemed
from trouble and gathered in from the lands, from the east
and from the west, from the north and from the south.

Psalm 107:2–3

Dear Lord God, I rejoice that people from every land and of every nation sing your praises. We are all united in our love for you and in our deep appreciation for the fact that you have redeemed us and made us your beloved children. Thank you for being our God and heavenly Father. Amen.

# OCTOBER 22

You have turned my mourning into dancing;
you have taken off my sackcloth
and clothed me with joy.

Psalm 30:11

Almighty Lord, I recall that you are the one
who made the seasons of the earth, which so aptly
reflect the seasons of my own life. From within times
of mourning, it seems as if things will never be different, that my heart will remain frozen with grief
and clouded over with pain. But each successive
day moves me steadily, though often impercepti-
bly, toward a new season of heart, soul, and mind.

Thank you for
your sure and gen-
tle ways that teach
me—when I've
forgotten how—to
dance once again.

Though my heart is full of pain
and sorrow, I will rejoice in the
Lord, for he is my God.

# OCTOBER 23

I will call to mind the deeds of the Lord; I will remember
your wonders of old. I will meditate on all your work,
and muse on your mighty deeds.

Psalm 77:11–12

As I think back through my life, I see many times when you, my supreme ruler, stepped in to make things happen. Sometimes it was obvious that you were acting with miraculous power, but not always. Some of your deeds were more subtle than that. Only in hindsight do I see that you were involved. Maybe at the time I thought I was just lucky, or that I had achieved something through my own brilliance. But now I see that you were there all the time, behind the scenes, orchestrating events, bringing the right people into my life at the right time, and empowering me to do what needed to be done. Thank you for your intervention. Thank you for all the great things you have done in my life.

God moves in a mysterious way,
his wonders to perform.

—William Cowper

# OCTOBER 24

Light dawns for the righteous,
and joy for the upright in heart.

Psalm 97:11

*W*hen the last sea is sailed and the last shallow
   charted,
When the last field is reaped and the last harvest
   stored,
When the last fire is out and the last guest departed,
Grant the last prayer that I shall pray,
Be good to me, O Lord!

—John Masefield,
*D'Avalos' Prayer*

The day that dawns in heaven for me will never know a sunset. In its eternal light, I will always live and rejoice without fear or pain or dread or sorrow or worry, with no shadow of death lurking and looming anymore. I shall soar in unmitigated joy and then light in pure peace and sing clearly and dance freely as I was created to do. I will be united at last with the love of my life and never again be separated from him nor from any of those who have loved him on earth. And so shall we ever be with the Lord, for the day that dawns in heaven for us will never know a sunset.

# OCTOBER 25

For a thousand years in your sight are like yesterday
when it is past, or like a watch in the night.

Psalm 90:4

*I* want your perspective on life, Lord. I want to take the large view. I fret so much about momentary things, but if I get the big picture will I see what's really important? Let me invest my life in things that matter—relationships, worship, using the gifts you've given me to return glory to you. I want to connect each day to eternity.

# OCTOBER 26

It is good to give thanks to the Lord...to declare your
steadfast love in the morning, and your faithfulness by night.

Psalm 92:1–2

*Most* holy Lord, in the quiet and solitude of a sleepless night, I have the opportunity to turn my nocturnal thoughts toward you. Let it be that even this night I will find the comfort of your presence and be thankful for the gifts of the day—even of the moment. May I commune with you in a tenderhearted return of blessing for blessing.

# OCTOBER 27

It is in vain that you rise up early
and go late to rest, eating the bread of anxious toil;
for he gives sleep to his beloved.

Psalm 127:2

*D*ear Lord, too often I can go to extremes— rigors you never intend for me—in my attempts to make my ends meet or to secure my position in this life. It's painfully ironic that at these times I am most prone to put off praying and seeking meaningful fellowship with you. Forgive me for defaulting to self-reliance, for thinking that it's all up  to me. Help me trust you so much that I will turn my back on worry and anxiety and, instead, spend time with you, get the rest I need, and allow you to be my source of strength and wisdom.

Sometimes getting a good night's sleep is
the most God-honoring thing we can do.

# OCTOBER 28

Our steps are made firm by the Lord, when he delights in our way;
though we stumble, we shall not fall headlong,
for the Lord holds us by the hand.

Psalm 37:23–24

Step by step you help me go.
Step by step I learn and grow.
Step by step you guide me well.
Step by—oops, I nearly fell.
Step by step you take delight
To pick me up and make things right.
Step by step and hand in hand
With you, along the path you've planned.

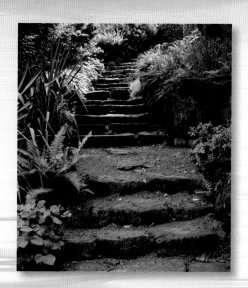

Since we live by the Spirit,
let us keep in step with the Spirit.

—Galatians 5:25 (NIV)

# OCTOBER 29

The ordinances of the Lord are true
and righteous altogether.

Psalm 19:9

Great God, you spoke the universe into being. Ever since, you've been speaking the light into our lives. I thank you for being a God who communicates. You have spoken to us through the prophets and apostles, and your Spirit brings the scriptures to life in our hearts. Your words are sweet to me. Keep speaking to me, dear Lord. I am listening.

# OCTOBER 30

The Lord is near to the brokenhearted,
and saves the crushed in spirit.

Psalm 34:18

In the middle of my pain, loving Father, sometimes there are no words I can bring to you—only groans of anguish, tears of sorrow, and the silence of suffering. But your presence has its own language of communion with my broken spirit. You don't despise my grief; you share in it with me. Thank you for always being here with me no matter what.

# OCTOBER 31

For he will command his angels concerning you to guard you
in all your ways. On their hands they will bear you up,
so that you will not dash your foot against a stone.

Psalm 91:11–12

*I* don't know much about angels, Lord,
But I'm really glad they're around
Rendering timely help.
I don't think I've ever seen one, Lord,
Which is just as well, because they'd
Surely scare me silly.
I don't want to worship angels, Lord,
Because they are all just
Servants like me.
But thank you for their help, Lord.

The tempter quoted scripture to Jesus,
trying to persuade him to jump off the
temple roof. Jesus replied with another verse,
forbidding the testing of God. Don't be
foolhardy about playing with danger, just
because you trust God to rescue you.

# NOVEMBER 1

For he did not despise or abhor the affliction of
the afflicted; he did not hide his face from me,
but heard when I cried to him.

Psalm 22:24

*D*ear Lord, I'm grateful for your compassion
and mercy. When I'm in need, you don't scold or
lecture, but you welcome me with open arms. Please
fill my heart with that kind of love, so I can do the
same for others. Often I run away from people
in need, fearing some entanglement and worried
that they'll need more than I can give. Or I judge
them, assuming they've brought their problems on

themselves. Give me
the sense of mercy that
pushes past those obsta-
cles and help me truly
love others in your holy
name, I pray.

"Lord, when was it that we saw you
hungry and gave you food, or thirsty
and gave you something to drink? . . . "
And the king will answer them, "Truly I
tell you, just as you did it to one of the
least of these who are members of my
family, you did it to me."

—Matthew 25:37, 40

# NOVEMBER 2

The heavens are the work of your hands. They will perish, but you
endure; ... You change them like clothing, and they pass away;
but you are the same, and your years have no end.

Psalm 102:25–27

*H*oly Creator, I look at
an ocean and I marvel. I see
a mountain and I say, "That's
really something!" The sheer
magnitude of that yet small
part of creation is awesome
to me. I see a canyon cut by
a river and I delight in your
artistry. But what is truly
amazing is that you outlast
all of these majestic master-

pieces. I gaze at the night sky with its untold stars,
and I exult in the wonder of your creation, but I
don't worship what you've made. I bow only before
you, the Creator.

Have you not known? Have you not heard?
The Lord is the everlasting God,
the Creator of the ends of the earth.
He does not faint or grow weary;
his understanding is unsearchable.

—Isaiah 40:28

# NOVEMBER 3

Take delight in the Lord,
and he will give you the desires of your heart.

Psalm 37:4

When was the last time I delighted in you, my Lord? Everything about you delights me—even the fact that you sometimes correct me, because I know you care for me. There will be reasons today for me to delight in you, as well. Help me not miss them, for *you* are the deepest desire of my heart.

# NOVEMBER 4

Teach me your way, O Lord, and lead me
on a level path because of my enemies.

Psalm 27:11

Dear Lord, because I get tripped up so easily, please stay close beside me. When I interact with others in my daily work, give me a wise head and a caring heart. When I spend time with my family, show me how to serve them best. When I face temptation, show me a way out. I know it's easy to fall; please keep me upright.

# NOVEMBER 5

I have been young, and now am old,
yet I have not seen the righteous forsaken
or their children begging bread.

Psalm 37:25

Through the years, supreme Lord, you have
provided. I thank you for that. You have proven

faithful again and again. I'm
not just talking about material things—food, clothing, a
home, and a job. You provide
such blessings according to
your wisdom, but, more than
that, you provide strength to get us through tough
times, you provide faith to focus on your spiritual
blessings, and you provide joy in relationships with
you and your people. Your promise is clear: A family that bases its life on your righteous love will not
be forsaken. You will bless them with your spiritual
blessings from generation to generation.

The best blessing that parents give their
children is an honest, living faith. Don't
hide flaws, market the faith, or look only
at the bright side. It is the stark reality of
God's presence that will win them.

# NOVEMBER 6

Happy are those who live in your house, ever singing your praise. Happy are those whose strength is in you, in whose heart are the highways to Zion.

Psalm 84:4–5

There's a highway in my heart, dear Lord, and it heads right to your home. When I need comfort, I go to you. When I need wisdom, I go to you. When I need courage or forgiveness or creativity, I hop on that highway and head in your direction. You are always there to meet me. Thank you, my Lord, for all you mean to me.

A voice cries out: "In the wilderness prepare the way of the Lord, make straight in the desert a highway for our God."

—Isaiah 40:3

# NOVEMBER 7

Come, O children, listen to me;
I will teach you the fear of the Lord.

Psalm 34:11

What does it mean to "fear" you, Lord? Yes, I am in awe of your power. Your holiness humbles me. You are God, and I know I am not. But my shrinking back is overcome by my attraction to you. This is how I "fear" you, by paying attention to you every day, living out my love for you.

# NOVEMBER 8

Help us, O God of our salvation, for the glory of your name;
deliver us, and forgive our sins, for your name's sake.

Psalm 79:9

Lord Jesus, please help me to always pray to you in repentant humility. I belong to you and am identified with you. Moreover, I am in need of your daily help. O, how I need you! Be pleased to glorify yourself today through the ways you bring salvation to me.

# NOVEMBER 9

We ponder your steadfast love, O God,
in the midst of your temple.

Psalm 48:9

*Y*our Word reminds me that my body is the temple of your Holy Spirit and that you dwell within me. It is from within this "temple," dear Lord, that I find myself thinking about your love. I remember how you have revealed your love for me time and again in the many ways you have cared for me. You

are my provision with your healing, protection, salvation, comfort, peace, forgiveness, kindness, goodness, gentleness, and faithfulness. There are so many ways you have made it clear to me that you love me. As I continue pondering your great love, make me aware of how I can show that love to those around me.

Love is simply an idea until it is put into action; we can say "I love you" as many times as we'd like, but until we act in love, our words are just sounds, clanging cymbals (read 1 Corinthians 13).

# NOVEMBER 10

But who can detect their errors? Clear me from hidden faults. . . .
[D]o not let them have dominion over me. Then I shall be blameless,
and innocent of great transgression.

Psalm 19:12–13

*F*ather in Heaven! Reawaken conscience in our
breast. Make us bend the ear of the spirit to Thy
voice, so that we may perceive Thy will for us in
its clear purity as it is in Heaven, pure of our false
worldly wisdom, unstifled by the voice of passion;
keep us vigilant.

—Søren Kierkegaard,
"To Know Thy Will"

We can become unaware of (or grow calloused to)
things that have crept into our lives over time—
sinful thoughts, attitudes, and actions—that work
against our relationship with God. That's why
self-examination under the direction of God's Spirit
can be vitally important to our spiritual growth.

# NOVEMBER 11

Happy are those who consider the poor;
the Lord delivers them in the day of trouble.

Psalm 41:1

You have told us, great Lord, to love our neighbors as ourselves. So help me, loving Father, to remember the poor—whether they are poor in finances, abilities, social graces, health, or any other kind of poverty. Remind me of how Jesus walked and talked and ministered to those in need, and by your Spirit, lead me in doing as Jesus has done.

# NOVEMBER 12

For who in the skies can be compared to the Lord?
Who among the heavenly beings is like the Lord?

Psalm 89:6

O Lord, no one compares to you! But all of this makes me think about how I relate to those with other beliefs. Please, Lord, help me speak the truth in love, being both wise and caring, while being honest about my faith but respectful of others.

# NOVEMBER 13

For the Lord is a great God,
and a great King above all gods.

Psalm 95:3

*O*ur God, God of all humanity,
God of heaven and earth, seas and rivers,
God of sun and moon, of all the stars,
God of high mountain and lowly valley,
God over heaven, and in heaven, and under heaven.
You have a dwelling in heaven and earth and sea
    and in all things that are in them.
You inspire all things, bring all things to life.
You are over all things, you support all things.
You make the light of the sun to shine,
You surround the moon and the stars,
You have made wells in the arid earth,
    placed dry islands in the sea.
Your Son is co-eternal with you,
And the Holy Spirit breathes in you.

—based on a prayer by Patrick of Ireland

Indeed he is not far from each one of us.
For "In him we live and move
and have our being."

—Acts 17:27–28

# NOVEMBER 14

Happy are those who make the Lord their trust,
who do not turn to the proud,
to those who go astray after false gods.

Psalm 40:4

*P*recious Lord, there are various "false gods" in this world, and I'll admit that I have strayed after some of them. Money is a big one. I keep thinking that my problems will be solved if I can just get enough money, but that's not true, is it? I chase after pleasure and success and entertainment as if

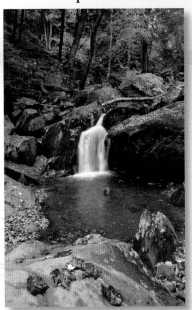

they gave my life meaning. My house, my car, or what is in my closet might as well be "graven images." But you continue to remind me that these things don't bring ultimate satisfaction. You are the only God worth trusting. I find fulfillment only in you.

You shall have no other gods before me.

—Exodus 20:3

# NOVEMBER 15

I lie down and sleep;
I wake again, for the Lord sustains me.

Psalm 3:5

At last! What a day it has been! I thought I'd never get to this moment, dear Lord. Thank you for the ways you were there for me today. I really sensed your presence throughout the day. Please give me a good night's sleep. Amen.

# NOVEMBER 16

The Lord has been mindful of us...he will bless those who fear the Lord, both small and great.

Psalm 115:12–13

May the wind be always at your back,
May the sun shine warm upon your face,
The rains fall soft upon your fields,
And until we meet again,
May God hold you in the palm of His hand.

—Author unknown,
"An Irish Wish"

# NOVEMBER 17

The Lord sets the prisoners free; the Lord opens the eyes of the blind.
The Lord lifts up those who are bowed down;
the Lord loves the righteous.

Psalm 146:7–8

Consumed by frustration, boxed in at every
angle,
Unable to do what's necessary to get ahead,
Locked in bad relationships, caged by addictions,
I turn to you.
You set prisoners free.
Uncertain where to go next, learning little
from the past,
Gazing at a hazy future and glimpsing nothing,
Looking past the people who love me,
Extremely near-sighted, I see only myself,
But then I turn to you.
You open the eyes of the blind.
Thank you, Lord.

Blessed are the poor in spirit,
for theirs is the kingdom of heaven.

—Matthew 5:3

# NOVEMBER 18

We will not hide them from their children; we will tell to the coming generation the glorious deeds of the Lord, and his might, and the wonders that he has done.

Psalm 78:4

*S*ometimes I'm shy, almighty God, when it comes to talking about you. You know how much I treasure the relationship that you and I have, but it's a very personal thing. I don't want to be some know-it-all telling everybody else what to believe. Still, I  wish other people would share the joy of this relationship with me. I do want to pass the good news along to other generations of people, but sometimes I lack the courage. So I'm asking you, Lord, for the wisdom to know when to speak, for the love to speak warmly, and for the courage to overcome my fears.

Today is a great time to talk about the Lord. With the coming of winter, people need to hear about our Savior.

# NOVEMBER 19

May those who sow in tears
reap with shouts of joy.

Psalm 126:5

Thank you, almighty Father, for the times of joy after periods of pain and sorrow. When the dark times engulf me, please keep my heart faithful to you so that I will not miss the inevitable outcome of rejoicing. Let my love for you be tempered in the seasons of sorrow so that my joy in you may be made complete.

# NOVEMBER 20

Even though I walk through the darkest valley, I fear no evil;
for you are with me; your rod and your staff—
they comfort me.

Psalm 23:4

There have been scary times in my life, when I had to walk through some "dark valleys" of disease, disaster, and desertion. Yet in those situations, Lord, you have comforted me, assuring me that you are right beside me. Thank you, Lord.

# NOVEMBER 21

Know that the Lord is God.
It is he that made us, and we are his;
we are his people, and the sheep of his pasture.

Psalm 100:3

*M*y precious Lord, what does it mean to *know* that you are God? The psalm for today gives me some clues: to remember that I'm not my own, that I belong to you, and that you made me. That's a start. I'll begin there, Lord, and thank you for making me. I'm thankful that I am one of your "sheep" and that you are such a kind and good shepherd, who with wisdom and patience tends to all that

pertains to my life. You are God, indeed. Help me often pause to remember it so that I won't get off track and wander from your kind and perfect purposes for my life.

I am the good shepherd. I know my own and my own know me, just as the Father knows me and I know the Father. And I lay down my life for the sheep.

John 10:14–15

# NOVEMBER 22

O satisfy us early with thy mercy;
that we may rejoice and be glad all our days.
Psalm 90:14 (KJV)

Your mercy amazes me, heavenly Father. I am in awe of your capacity to forgive. I know I have disappointed you, and I deserve nothing from you but judgment. Instead, you show mercy to me. You reach out with your steadfast love and welcome me back into your good graces. I thank you for  this undeserved favor. I praise you for your overwhelming grace. And I pray for your power to walk in holiness.

For by grace you have been saved through faith, and this is not your own doing; it is the gift of God—not the result of works, so that no one may boast. For we are what he has made us, created in Christ Jesus for good works, which God prepared beforehand to be our way of life.

—Ephesians 2:8–10

# NOVEMBER 23

Gladden the soul of your servant,
for to you, O Lord, I lift up my soul.

Psalm 86:4

Lord God, winter is not far off. Days of cold and waiting lie ahead. So please go before me and lead me forward with a glad heart. Let me begin today, Lord, by lifting up my soul to you to be made glad, not by my circumstances, but by my relationship with you, and just by the fact that you have made me and you love me.

# NOVEMBER 24

He fulfills the desire of all who fear him;
he also hears their cry, and saves them.

Psalm 145:19

My Lord, I desire that your kingdom come to flourish in the hearts of those who seek you and that your will be carried out here on earth in the way it is carried out in heaven. I desire to honor and glorify you all the days of my life and into eternity. In your name, I pray. Amen.

# NOVEMBER 25

Enter his gates with thanksgiving,
and his courts with praise.
Give thanks to him, bless his name.

Psalm 100:4

*I* want to come to you, into your presence, with praise on my lips right now, my Lord. How well you deserve it! How sad it would be for me to sweep aside your many blessings to focus only on the problems of the day! I won't do that. Instead, I'll praise you. There will be time for addressing the concerns I have, but I will set my soul and my lips free to thank you and to bless your name.

Gratitude is the most exquisite form of courtesy.

—Jacques Maritain,
*Reflections on America*

# NOVEMBER 26

Posterity will serve him; future generations will be told about the Lord, and proclaim his deliverance to a people yet unborn, saying that he has done it.

Psalm 22:30–31

Heavenly Father, let my life count for you, not only today and tomorrow, but also in the years to come. Can I leave a legacy that will inspire people long after I've gone? I'm not looking for personal fame here, but I want to serve you fully. So let me cast my vision forward. How will my devotion to you affect the next generation as well as the succeeding generations? Use me, dear Lord, to bring the dynamic reality of you to the children in my life, not only teaching them but also empowering them to serve you in the future. It is my humble prayer that "people yet unborn" might be brought closer to you.

Keep these words that I am commanding you today in your heart. Recite them to your children and talk about them when you are at home and when you are away, when you lie down and when you rise.

—Deuteronomy 6:6–7

# NOVEMBER 27

O Lord, open my lips,
and my mouth will declare your praise.

Psalm 51:15

*S*ometimes I just don't feel like praising you,
heavenly Father, even though I know you deserve my
praise 24/7. When my soul meets the idea of rejoicing with a grumpy attitude, please wash over my sour
soul with a fresh awareness of your greatness and
goodness. Open my mouth by opening my heart
and filling it with sincere praise once again.

# NOVEMBER 28

I praise you, for I am fearfully and wonderfully made.
Wonderful are your works; that I know very well.

Psalm 139:14

*I* can look at a sunset and marvel at your
handiwork. But then I notice I can get a much closer
view of your artistry any time I want it. You have
created *me*. My body and mind contain intricate
patterns wonderful to behold, and you created my
spirit to commune with yours. Lord, I thrill to think
of all you have made, including myself.

# NOVEMBER 29

Then I acknowledged my sin to you, and I did not hide my iniquity;
I said, "I will confess my transgressions to the Lord,"
and you forgave the guilt of my sin.

Psalm 32:5

*I* am a sinner. You and I both know that, Lord. There are all sorts of self-help books that wouldn't want me to say that. I'm "misunderstood" or "guilt-afflicted" or "not living up to my potential." But the simple truth is this: I've done wrong. In my thoughts and deeds, in my actions and attitudes toward others, toward myself, and toward you, I have disobeyed  you, and I'm sorry. But the story doesn't end there. You offer forgiveness for my sins, no matter how heinous they are. You restore my relationship with you. You wipe the slate clean. Thank you, beloved Lord. I bless you from the depths of my renewed heart.

To err is human, to forgive divine.

—Alexander Pope

# NOVEMBER 30

The idols of the nations are silver and gold, the work of human hands. They have mouths, but they do not speak; ... Those who make them and all who trust them shall become like them.

Psalm 135:15–16, 18

My Lord, idols come in many flawed forms. They may be a celebrity, a dream job, a big house, or even an unhealthy relationship. If this is true with me, reveal that idol to me, humble my pride, and draw me close to you. Lord, only you are worthy of my worship. Please forgive my wandering heart and embrace me once again. I want to worship only you.

You shall love the Lord your God with all your heart, and with all your soul, and with all your might.

—Deuteronomy 6:5

# DECEMBER 1

How very good and pleasant it is
when kindred live together in unity!

Psalm 133:1

*I*n this season of family get-
togethers, my heavenly Father,
I thank you for the good things
about my family. And, Lord,
where there are family challenges and strife, I pray that

you would intervene. Please soften hearts, change
minds, grant grace and forgiveness . . . even miracles!
Heal our broken relationships, dear Father, and protect our healthy ones. Let unity ultimately prevail—
but not a thin, superficial unity that could break
at any moment. Please forge an unbreakable unity
within our hearts by your righteousness and peace.

Grace, forgiveness, and love are essential
ingredients for unity among believers.

# DECEMBER 2

Prove me, O Lord, and try me; test my heart and mind.
For your steadfast love is before my eyes,
and I walk in faithfulness to you.

Psalm 26:2–3

*M*erciful Lord, I understand the concept of testing. I tie a knot and yank on it to make sure it will hold. I have vivid memories of difficult exams in school that seemed to turn my brain inside out and shake it to see what would come out. I don't have a lot of experience with smelting, but I know that metal goes into the furnace and it comes out stronger. I get it. Being tested is good for us. But it's

still tough to go through. I don't know what kind of test you're putting me through right now, but I hope it's over soon. And I hope I'll pass the test and that I'll come out of it stronger, wiser, and closer to you. But I have to tell you, I'm not sure I'm going to make it. Please, God, help me!

[God] knows the way that I take; when he
has tested me, I will come forth as gold.

—Job 23:10 (NIV)

# DECEMBER 3

As far as the east is from the west,
so far he removes our transgressions from us.

Psalm 103:12

Most Holy God, I'm amazed by your capacity for forgiveness. We both know that I have wronged you. I come before you as a sinner, dependant on your mercy. Thankfully, you lift me up and wipe the slate clean. Thank you, my dear Lord. And please give me that same ability to forgive others. Amen.

# DECEMBER 4

Trust in him at all times, O people;
pour out your heart before him.

Psalm 62:8

Dear Lord, sometimes my heart isn't in my prayers. And when I think about how a human relationship would fare if there was just cognitive communication with no heart-level interaction, I see my deep need to engage my heart in our relationship. Help me as I seek to open up to you in the days ahead.

# DECEMBER 5

I love the Lord, because he has heard my voice and my supplications. Because he inclined his ear to me, therefore I will call on him as long as I live.

Psalm 116:1–2

My heart is filled with love for you, dear Lord. I can't begin to express the depth of my feelings. You have created me and re-created me. You have forgiven me and saved me. You give me joy each day and hope for the days ahead. When I call upon you in a time of need, you hear my prayer. You come close to me and whisper the assurance of your love. Thank you, Lord, for listening to me. I love you.

God is love, and those who abide in love abide in God, and God abides in them.

—1 John 4:16

# DECEMBER 6

As for me, I am poor and needy,
but the Lord takes thought for me.
You are my help and my deliverer.

Psalm 40:17

*G*reat God, I thank you for the many times you
have met my needs—not only material needs but
emotional, relational, and spiritual needs as well.
Sometimes with near-miracles, but usually in sub-
tler ways, you work your wonders, and I have been
blessed. I thank you for the care you've shown
to me, and I ask you to help me care for others.
Give me eyes to see the needs around me and the
strength to do what I can to show your love.

My God will fully satisfy every need of yours
according to his riches in glory in Christ Jesus.

—Philippians 4:19

# DECEMBER 7

Surely the righteous shall give thanks to your name;
the upright shall live in your presence.

Psalm 140:13

Thank you for the righteousness I have in you, Lord Jesus. You have granted me the status of a righteous person in your redemption, and you are transforming me in righteous living as I walk with you by your Spirit. To live with you, now and forever, is the crowning glory of this journey.

# DECEMBER 8

Better is a little that the righteous person has
than the abundance of many wicked.

Psalm 37:16

Today, Lord, I want to focus on my true wealth. This can't be measured in dollars and cents but rather in love and grace. You, Lord, have showered abundant blessings upon me. Just to know you is a great reward, and I am truly grateful.

# DECEMBER 9

Why should I fear in times of trouble, when the iniquity of my persecutors surrounds me, those who trust in their wealth and boast of the abundance of their riches?

Psalm 49:5–6

*H*ow easily I get swept into the love of money! Lord, I know that you are all I need. I'd rather have you than all the wealth on earth, but lately I've been worrying about financial matters. All over the news media, I hear the voices of those who trust in their riches, and I'm tempted to join them, to want more,

and to fear having less. But then I hear your gentle wooing. You are truly enough for me, dear Lord. I need not fret. I can trust you to provide.

Therefore I tell you, do not worry about your life, what you will eat or what you will drink, or about your body, what you will wear. Is not life more than food, and the body more than clothing? . . . But strive first for the kingdom of God and his righteousness, and all these things will be given to you as well.

—Matthew 6:25, 33

# DECEMBER 10

For every wild animal of the forest is mine, the cattle
on a thousand hills. I know all the birds of the air,
and all that moves in the field is mine.

Psalm 50:10–11

Although you have entrusted humanity with the care of your creation, heavenly Father, all of it still belongs to you. Remind me to be a good caretaker of all that you have entrusted to me in my corner of the world. Grant me your wisdom as I make choices about how to best tend those things in my care. Help me be diligent to do what is within my power to be a responsible tenant while I'm here. Bless and multiply the efforts of those who are doing good and honest work to care for your creation.

If your heart is straight with God, then
every creature will be to you a mirror of life
and a book of holy doctrine. No creature
is so little or so mean as not to show forth
and represent the goodness of God.

—Thomas à Kempis,
*The Imitation of Christ*

# DECEMBER 11

Blessed is the one who comes in the name of the Lord.
We bless you from the house of the Lord.

Psalm 118:26

*L*ord Jesus, I remember these words from the psalms that express the praise shouted at your triumphal entry. Every day, I seek your presence to steer me through my challenges. I need your assurance, your comfort, and your wisdom. So I bless you, dear Lord. Thank you for entering my life.

# DECEMBER 12

Happy are the people whose God is the Lord.

Psalm 144:15

*D*ear Lord, you are my greatest benefit and blessing. When I think of belonging to you, I get lost in the amazement of that thought. You have made me glad in your care. You have made me hope in your salvation. You have made me believe in your promises. You have made me to love you because you first loved me. What more could I want?

# DECEMBER 13

He covers the heavens with clouds,
prepares rain for the earth,
makes grass grow on the hills.

Psalm 147:8

My Creator, the more I know about creation, the more I want to praise you. You have made a universe that flows together in a beautiful way. The sun heats the earth, creating water vapor that forms clouds and returns to earth in the form of rain, which makes the grass grow, which feeds animals, and so on. It is a beautiful pattern—one that reflects your wisdom, power, and love. I hope I never again complain about the rain, because it's all part of the intricate design you have put in place.

Ever since the creation of the world his eternal power and divine nature, invisible though they are, have been understood and seen through the things he has made.

—Romans 1:20

# DECEMBER 14

We have heard with our ears, O God, our ancestors have
told us, what deeds you performed in their days,
in the days of old.

Psalm 44:1

Almighty Father, help me be faithful in telling the younger generation about you. Help me
not assume either that they know or that they don't
really care to hear about spiritual realities. Remind
me of the stories of good things you have done in
my life when I'm around
children, and even teens.
Then, I pray that you would
grant me a gift of articula-
tion so that I can communicate in ways that reach their
inner being and stir up a
longing to know you. May
there always be people in
each subsequent generation
who love to sing your praise.

We're on a "pay it forward" plan when
it comes to the gospel. Each successive
generation has passed on the Good
News to the next. We now have the
privilege of "paying it forward" to those
who will come after us.

274

# DECEMBER 15

I will praise the Lord as long as I live;
I will sing praises to my God all my life long.

Psalm 146:2

*E*ven if my ability to utter a sound gives way to silence in my old age, dear Lord, I ask that you would grant me grace to make music to you in my heart and mind and to praise you even when my life is coming to an end. By then I should have a treasure trove of memories of the way you've blessed my life. Amen.

# DECEMBER 16

O God, you know my folly;
the wrongs I have done are not hidden from you.

Psalm 69:5

*O* Father! Each wrong that I bring to you and confess, you readily forgive and begin the process of redemption. I'm deeply grateful for these miracles, but I pray that you would cause me to grow wiser from my mistakes and more faithful so I can walk in your righteousness.

# DECEMBER 17

May he grant you your heart's desire, and fulfill all your plans.
May we shout for joy over your victory,
and in the name of our God set up our banners.

Psalm 20:4–5

*I* pray today for those stepping out into new ventures, especially those who are seeking new ways to serve you. Go with them, Lord. Guide them in the planning process, and grant them success. Encourage them when things don't work out at first, and help them keep their heads when they encounter the first flush of success. Along with the psalmist, I want to "shout for joy" and wave flags to celebrate their victory. Please, Lord, honor the desires of your servants to serve you more effectively.

He brought me to the banqueting house, and his banner over me was love.

—Song of Solomon 2:4 (KJV)

# DECEMBER 18

The Lord says to my lord, "Sit at my right hand until
I make your enemies your footstool." The Lord sends
out from Zion your mighty scepter.

Psalm 110:1–2

*A* new king was born in Bethlehem, laid in a manger, announced by angels, and worshipped by wise men. Lord God, you handed authority to the Lord Jesus in order to accomplish a daring rescue mission. It's amazing, when I think about it, that you were venturing into enemy  territory. Earth was, and is, full of people who resent you, resist you, and reject you—and still you entrusted the royal child to this hurting planet. It's a magnificent story, and it makes me want to worship you even more. Amen

Jesus used this psalm to explain his
unique identity as both God and man,
since the Lord God was granting
authority to someone even King David
(the psalmist) called "my lord."

# DECEMBER 19

If my father and mother forsake me,
the Lord will take me up.

Psalm 27:10

*R*elationships are both beautiful and difficult. Today I bring before you my closest relationships. You understand the pleasure I draw from their love and also the anxiety. I ask you to stand behind these connections. Help us to listen to each other and to you. Give us patience, wisdom, and creativity. Share with us your secrets of sacrificial love.

# DECEMBER 20

Great is the Lord, and greatly to be praised;
his greatness is unsearchable.

Psalm 145:3

*D*ear Lord, I realize that the "unsearchableness" of your greatness isn't intended to discourage my searching for it. I'll keep searching as long as I live. Thank you for disclosing yourself in so many wonderful ways. You are a great God!

# DECEMBER 21

Bless the Lord, O you his angels, you mighty ones who
do his bidding, obedient to his spoken word.
Bless the Lord, all his hosts, his ministers that do his will.

Psalm 103:20–21

At this time of year, almighty Father, I think
of the angels who put this psalm into practice
one night in the skies over Bethlehem. They truly
blessed you, Lord, singing, "Glory to God in the
highest." What an amazing sight that must have
been! And how I'd love to hear the sounds of that
celestial choir! Maybe someday, when we're all in

heaven together, I'll ask them
for a repeat performance. Lord,
I thank you for the ministry of
those angels, who delivered to
humanity the most important
message ever.

Then an angel of the Lord stood before
them, and the glory of the Lord shone
around them, and they were terrified. But
the angel said to them, "Do not be afraid."

—Luke 2:9–10

# DECEMBER 22

Yet God my King is from of old,
working salvation in the earth.

Psalm 74:12

*H*ail the heavenly Prince of Peace!
Hail the Sun of Righteousness!
Light and life to all He brings,
Ris'n with healing in His wings.
Mild He lays His glory by,
Born that man no more may die.
Born to raise the sons of earth,
Born to give them second birth.
Hark! the herald angels sing,
"Glory to the newborn King!"

—Charles Wesley,
"Hark! The Herald Angels Sing"

"I am bringing you good news of great
joy for all the people: to you is born this
day in the city of David a Savior, who is
the Messiah, the Lord."

—Luke 2:10–11

# DECEMBER 23

Make vows to the Lord your God, and perform them;
let all who are around him bring gifts
to the one who is awesome.

Psalm 76:11

*W*hat gifts do I have to bring to you, most awesome Lord? Gold? Well, my accounts are limited. Frankincense and myrrh? I'm not sure how to get those things or how to give them. But I think you want more from me anyway. My attention? My creativity? The risks I take to love others? As people rush out to buy last-minute presents to put under

the tree, I want to give you something truly special. Tell me, Lord: What do you want for Christmas?

On entering the house, they saw the child with Mary his mother; and they knelt down and paid him homage. Then, opening their treasure chests, they offered him gifts of gold, frankincense, and myrrh.

—Matthew 2:11

# DECEMBER 24

Praise the Lord! Praise the Lord from the heavens;
praise him in the heights! Praise him, all his angels;
praise him, all his host!

Psalm 148:1–2

*A*ngels from the realms of glory,
  Wing your flight o'er all the earth;
Ye who sang creation's story,
  Now proclaim Messiah's birth.
Come and worship, come and worship.
  Worship Christ, the newborn King.
Shepherds, in the field abiding,
  Watching o'er your flocks by night,
God with us is now residing;
  Yonder shines the infant light:
Come and worship, come and worship.
  Worship Christ, the newborn King.

—James Montgomery,
"Angels from the Realms of Glory"

When they saw this, they made known
what had been told them about this
child; and all who heard it were amazed
at what the shepherds told them.

—Luke 2:17–18

# DECEMBER 25

I will tell of the decree of the Lord: He said to me,
"You are my son; today I have begotten you."

Psalm 2:7

Today we celebrate the birth of your only begotten Son, our Lord and Savior, Jesus Christ. The mystery of Christmas is deep and compelling—how and even why your Son was born a baby. For him to pour himself into human flesh, to become a baby, and to consent to be born in a stable—this is beyond our comprehension. It was an act of supreme love, and I praise you for it. When all the presents have been opened, when the feast is cleared away, when the shreds of wrapping paper are discarded, and when the sparkling lights are turned off, this will stay with me—the remarkable love of the one who made me.

What wondrous love is this
That caused the Lord of bliss
To bear the dreadful curse
For my soul.

—attributed to Alexander Means,
"What Wondrous Love Is This?"

# DECEMBER 26

When I am afraid, I put my trust in you. In God, whose word I praise,
in God I trust; I am not afraid; what can flesh do to me?

Psalm 56:3–4

*M*any times I have found, Lord God, that your
Word has shored up my faith when circumstances
have shaken me to the core. I praise you for your
Word, which is able to empower my faith.

# DECEMBER 27

Sing to the Lord, bless his name;
tell of his salvation from day to day.

Psalm 96:2

*T*here are so many ways your salvation comes
to me, my Savior. I truly can speak of it from day to
day. You protect me in the course of the day, often
in ways I don't see, but when I lie down, I feel safe
from harm at night because of your presence. Your
salvation surrounds me, Lord. And so, I shall speak
of it whenever and wherever I see or experience it.

# DECEMBER 28

God, your God, has anointed you with the oil of gladness beyond your companions; your robes are all fragrant with myrrh and aloes and cassia. From ivory palaces stringed instruments make you glad.

Psalm 45:7–8

*T*oday's psalm paints a royal portrait—a king enjoying palace life. I wonder if this is a glimpse of your heavenly life, before you came to earth to be born. If so, it's a stark con-trast to the stable. Fragrant robes replaced with swaddling clothes. Suddenly your "companions" are oxen and donkeys. This is what you gave up in order to save us. I love the fact that one of these royal scents is myrrh. The magi knew you were a king, and they offered a whiff of majesty. Lord Jesus, thank you for becoming one of us. In your precious name, I pray. Amen.

Christ Jesus . . . though he was in the form of God, did not regard equality with God as something to be exploited, but emptied himself, taking the form of a slave, being born in human likeness.

—Philippians 2:5–7

# DECEMBER 29

Sing to him a new song;
play skillfully on the strings, with loud shouts.

Psalm 33:3

*I* like the old songs, almighty God. I know how to sing those. The new ones shake me up with a new challenge, as well as a new blessing. Help me see your hand in the new things I don't yet understand and praise you for making all things—including my life—new and beautiful.

# DECEMBER 30

Will you not revive us again,
so that your people may rejoice in you?

Psalm 85:6

*T*he week between Christmas and New Year's Day is always an interesting time, dear Lord. In this in-between time I look to you for guidance. How will the blessings of Christmas take hold in my life? And how will I live out the truth of Christmas in the coming year?

# DECEMBER 31

Then we your people, the flock of your pasture,
will give thanks to you forever;
from generation to generation we will recount your praise.

Psalm 79:13

*D*ear Lord, as each year draws to a close, I begin to take a long look at myself. Where is my life headed? What am I accomplishing? And what will I leave behind when my time on earth is up? I'm grateful for the way you've worked in my life, but now I look to the next generation. Have I passed on any faith or wisdom to the younger set? Have I mentored anyone to take my place— whatever that place might be? Have I inspired the next generation to praise you? Lord, let this be the focus of the coming year for me. Let me pass forward your praises.

You then, my child, be strong in the grace that is in Christ Jesus; and what you have heard from me through many witnesses entrust to faithful people who will be able to teach others as well.

—2 Timothy 2:1–2

# ACKNOWLEDGMENTS